GIRL, WE NEED TO TALK

GIRL, WE NEED TO talk

THE MINISTER'S WIFE & HER STRUGGLES

BY WOMEN WHO'VE BEEN THERE

EDITED BY CHRIS McCURLEY

START2FINISH

ISBN-10: 1941972578
ISBN-13: 978-1941972571

Library of Congress Control Number: 2015933297

Published by Start2Finish Books
PO Box 660675 #54705
Dallas, TX 75266-0675
www.start2finish.org

Printed in the United States of America

Cover Design: Josh Feit, Evangela.com

CONTENTS

INTRODUCTION
Chris McCurley

Ministry is my second career. My first vocation was a teacher/coach in the public school system. Many would say I jumped out of the frying pan and into the fire by transitioning from coaching to preaching. There are some days when I would agree with that assessment, but I absolutely love being a preacher. The joy and benefits far outweigh the stresses and disappointments. It was not that way with coaching. I had reached the point where the thrill of victory did not override the agony of defeat. When that happens, it is time to move on. Thankfully, the opportunity to do ministry appeared, and I have never looked back.

Whether through coaching or preaching, I have found one thing to be constant: there will always be frustration. Defeat is even more agonizing now, but victory is all the sweeter. Besides, the victories always outnumber the defeats.

The struggles of a minister are real, and no one knows this better than a minister's wife. She stands by her husband's side, sharing in the successes and stresses, the triumphs and tragedies. She compliments him. She consoles him. She is the first to congratulate him when he hits a home run from the pulpit and the first to comfort him when he feels he has struck out. She feels the outpouring of love from church members, but also witnesses the ugliness of people who claim to love God. She rejoices with him and mourns with him. Truly, she sees it all. Most importantly, her husband knows he would be nothing without her. Through thick and thin, she stands by him even as he stands in the frying pan.

When legendary coach Pat Riley coached the Los Angeles Lakers, his team won four NBA Championships. In 1991, Riley took over as head coach for the New York Knicks. Although he inherited a team with a losing record, Riley was able to make them competitive again. He later went on to coach the Miami Heat and win a championship in 2006. Now he is president of the Heat and has overseen two more championships. Many have asked Pat Riley about the secret to his success, to which he has replied, "We measure areas of performance that are often ignored: jumping in pursuit of every rebound even if you don't get it, swatting at every pass, diving for loose balls, letting someone smash into you in order to draw a foul. Effort is what ultimately separates journeyman players from impact players. Knowing how well a player executes all these little things is the key to unlocking career-best performances."

The minister and his wife are also a team, and being a minister's wife often entails doing things that are easily ignored. While we are watching the slam dunk, we miss the four other men on the court who made it possible. There are always things that people do not pay attention to, things that are vital to the work of the home and the church. It is the execution of the "little" things that produces the key to long-term success.

I once thought being a coach's wife had to be one of the

most difficult roles a woman could fill. What must it be like to sit in the stands and put on a smile of support when the team loses? When everyone around you questions your husband's decisions and mistakes? However, filling the role of a preacher's wife can be twice as uncomfortable. There are times when she may feel like an outcast, like she is not living up to her role and responsibility of being a minister's wife. She can easily feel guilty, like she is not measuring up. And, many times, she suffers in silence as the neglected and forgotten partner.

What follows is a book of hope. It is a book for the neglected and forgotten partner who needs encouragement of her own. This book will help guide, strengthen, and equip the minister's wife to face the future and the trials therein.

Ten godly women have contributed their wisdom, their experience, and their encouragement to this project. Each of them is a minister's wife who knows, all too well, what it is like to stand in the frying pan. They are women of integrity who have felt the rush of victory and the sting of defeat. They know what it means to be an unsung hero. They undertake the jobs that are so often ignored and complete them with grace. Each of these women are well acquainted with the sometimes thankless position of being a minister's wife.

Whether it is living in the fish bowl, supporting your husband, making friends, or honoring confidentiality, being a minister's wife can be both fulfilling and troubling. There may be times when you think about quitting. Don't. Numerous ministers' wives have been where you are, only to discover that the number of faith victories far outweigh the defeats. And I am grateful for the efforts of these women and many others who stand beside the pulpit in silent support. I pray that the words that follow will be a blessing to all who read this book.

1

LIVING IN A FISH BOWL
Donna Faughn

One of my doctors has a huge aquarium in his waiting room full of beautiful fish. While waiting for our appointments, I often pass the time watching those fish swim around in their segregated environment. They are beautiful, graceful creatures who seem oblivious to everyone watching them. As a child, I had a small fish bowl and a goldfish who, sadly, didn't have a very long life. When I first got him (or maybe her), I spent lots of time watching him swim happily around and around in that small little home. Sometimes he would come right up to the glass, and it always seemed like he was observing the world outside that little bowl while I was looking in.

As a preacher's wife, I have felt as if I was living in a clear glass fish bowl. It often seems that rather than observing what's on the outside, everyone else is observing what's on the inside of my little home. I have felt as if my family was on constant display and held to a standard no one could ever achieve.

All in all, I've lived in three fish bowls as a minister's wife. The first was a very small bowl that required a great deal of work to make it liveable. We lived there for seven years. The second bowl was a little larger and fairly new, and we lived in that one for eleven years. The third was a huge bowl that had been terribly neglected and needed some tender loving care. It was the only one of the three that belonged to the church when we moved in, but we have since purchased it from the church. We have lived in it now, and rather happily, for almost fifteen years.

I tell you about these three bowls to let you know that I have had some experience living in a fish bowl. I know what it is like to have everyone watching you, assessing your choices, and judging your mistakes. I've learned some very valuable lessons while living the fish bowl life, and I want to share some of them with you. I want to talk about what it's like living in a fish bowl— or maybe more appropriately—a glass house.

WHO OWNS YOUR GLASS HOUSE?

It may be that your home is owned by the church, and you are allowed to live there while your husband is the resident preacher. How you approach this arrangement can make all the difference in the world.

As I said earlier, I have only lived in one church "parsonage." It was a wreck when we took the job, and the congregation was small and not very stable financially. Realizing funds would be limited for making the house liveable, I knew I should be careful about how I worded what we needed to have done. Remembering what James says about the tongue and the damage it can do (Jas. 3:5) came in very handy at this point. If I had started talking about how terrible the house was and how much work it needed, we would have started on very shaky ground with our congregation. Instead, I spoke of the house's potential and what might help make it more liveable, which got us off to a much better beginning. Also, donating a great deal of our own "sweat equity" helped the members see that we wanted to live and work with them. Some of my favorite memories of that time are of the people who worked by our side as we cleaned, painted, and repaired our home. We grew closer together each day; we worked, talked, laughed, and ate together. They saw us as co-laborers—not demanding overlords—and thus we formed a deep bond of mutual respect.

Maybe you were able to purchase your own glass house (something I highly recommend, if you can afford it). Since that time, we have bought that house we worked so hard to repair. It has such wonderful memories of happy times with our church's members, some of whom have gone on to their reward. It has so much of us in it that it truly is home. Whether you own your own glass house or live in the church's glass house, there are some things I feel will help you as a preacher's wife. Some of those things have to do with the actual house itself, while others deal with your working relationship with the congregation. I think all of them will be helpful as you journey down this path of life you have chosen.

YOU ARE VISIBLE!

It's hard to hide when you live in a glass house. People are watching you: how you look, how you act, how your children act, and what you say are all observed and analyzed. For some reason, my mind goes to a song, "There's an All Seeing Eye Watching You," and the line "...watching you, watching you, every day mind the course you pursue." This seems to be one of the most difficult aspects of being the preacher's family. Our husbands are so visible that we make the assumption, and rightly so, that we are also visible.

The problem comes when we focus on this visibility and make it larger than it really is. When we allow ourselves to make assumptions concerning what people are thinking about us or our children, problems may arise. The concept of constantly being in the public eye puts more pressure on ourselves than is actually necessary until we try to become someone we're not.

I remember a teaching of Jesus found in Matt. 5:16, "Let your light shine before others, so that they may see your good works and give glory to your Father who is in heaven." When I remove the focus from myself (and my children) and recognize that my life needs to reflect the light of Jesus, I don't have a problem with living in a house where I am visible. There may be those who will still be watching my every move, but if I focus on living the way Jesus would have me live, then I will have no problem with being visible.

We are visible, yes, but what exactly do we communicate to those who are viewing us? So much is communicated without ever saying a word. Does our face show we are happy to be where we are, or does it appear to others as though we wish we were anywhere else? I've known some preachers' wives who seemed to communicate that the congregation owed them something, or that the members weren't quite up to their level, be it physically or spiritually. Jesus never portrayed this to others, so we most certainly shouldn't either. Our expressions and actions ought to express that we love and appreciate them. When you become part of a congregation, you join another part of God's family. Let them see your happiness and joy over being a part of their congregation.

Since people are watching you, be sure you present to them what Jesus would have you present.

DON'T THROW STONES AT OTHERS!

Common sense should tell us that when you live in a glass house, you shouldn't throw stones at anyone! How we treat others is very important, regardless of how they treat us. Trust me, when you throw stones at others, you may get some thrown back!

Have you ever said, or heard someone else say, something like this: "I know she means well, but..." or "I'm not supposed to tell, but..."? How about: "She may think her children are perfect, but..." or "She always has to have things her way"? The list could go on and on, couldn't it?

No good can be accomplished by such statements, whether you are the one saying such things or if another member of the congregation is saying such things to you. Either way, no good can come from it. Gossip, backbiting, innuendo, and unkind remarks have no place in the Christian's life. These are the tools of Satan and can most certainly be used to hurt, weaken, divide, or even destroy a congregation.

Unfortunately, there will be times when stones will be thrown at you and your family, even as you try to live a life pleasing to God. Even when you have done nothing to deserve it, stones can still be thrown at you. Remember, you are visible.

The little town in which I grew up had an old button factory. It had closed its doors many years earlier, but the buildings were still there. Those buildings were full of windows, hundreds of them. Some of the kids in town threw stones at the windows just to break them—just for the fun of it.

I've known some people like that in the church. They throw stones for some unknown reason. It may be jealousy, instability, envy, curiosity, or any number of other reasons, but it taught me a valuable lesson. Satan is alive and well. He will use any method he can to cause me to stumble and fall in my Christian walk.

While I can't control what others do or say, I can control how I react to them. How we treat others, by our actions and through our words, is a reflection of what is in our hearts. I am sure all of us want our hearts to be pure before God. Don't be guilty of throwing stones, because there is always the chance that some will be thrown back at you!

A GLASS HOUSE IS UNIQUE, SO SHARE IT WITH OTHERS!

Hospitality is so important, but it is much more than just opening up your home to others. A couple of women in the Bible quickly come to my mind as I think about this. Lydia opened her home to Paul and those who were with him after she and her household had been converted to Christ. Mary and Martha were also very hospitable to Jesus. Many lessons have been taught about how differently they handled hospitality, but the bottom line is that they invited him into their home, and he felt welcome there. Hospitality is offering a welcome to those who pass through our door. It is a comfortable place to visit, an openness in our attitude, and happiness that they have come our way.

I was told of a preacher and his family who lived in a community for a few years, but never had anyone in their home. Along with that little tidbit, I was told that they always had all of the blinds closed, and the window in the front door covered over with aluminum foil. I don't really know why I needed to know those things unless it was so I could use it here as an example. I don't know the reasons for closing the blinds and blacking out the window on the front door, but I sure know what kind of impression it gave to those in the congregation—"You're not welcome in our home." Regardless of whether this was truly how the preacher or his family felt, it still contributed to a short stay for that preacher and his family.

When we invite others into our home, we are inviting them into our lives as well. They see how we live and the things that are important to us. They see the family pictures and the little trinkets that decorate our home. It opens a door for sharing your family and hearing stories about theirs. Hospitality allows us to share on a more personal level because we have taken the time to share not only our home but our lives.

Have you ever been invited into the home of someone who has it all, materially speaking? It's beautifully decorated, modern, spotless, and you were a little bit afraid to touch anything. Sometimes that type of home leaves us feeling as though the beauty of the home is more important than the relationships between people. This type of house is a showpiece, not a home; it is an exhibition of the life they want you to see, not who they truly are.

Maybe you've been invited into the home of someone who actually lives there. The furniture is worn, but comfortable. The house is neat, but not spotless. The kitchen looks well used, and family pictures are found in every room. You come away with the feeling that relationships between people are more important than the surroundings.

Whatever your glass house is like, do your best to make it a place that welcomes all who pass through the door. Let them know that you care about and are interested in a relationship with them.

WINDEX IS IMPORTANT WHEN YOU LIVE IN A GLASS HOUSE

This is a tough one to talk about because the opinions about proper housekeeping are varied. When I teach Tit. 2 to younger women, I try to stress all of the things Paul told Titus to teach the older women—how to behave, how to control themselves, and what to teach younger women. We are all familiar with the curriculum older women are instructed to teach the youth—love for their husbands and children, to be self-controlled, pure, kind, and submissive. Right in the middle of that list is one more quality that women should possess: "keepers at home" (KJV), "homemakers" (NKJV), and "working at home" (ESV).

This is a very sticky subject and ruffles plenty of feathers any time you mention it! I understand what it is like to try to keep a tidy house when you have younger children, and your schedule is so full. I also realize that spiritual growth and work for the Lord are of the utmost importance. I do not believe these things are mutually exclusive. I feel like we are falling down on the job in many homes when we don't keep our house presentable and train our children in its importance. Children love to help when they are little. What better time to begin training them about being stewards of what God has given us? Their beds may not be made to your standard, but they are learning. They won't dust like you do, but they are learning. They can't cook like you can, or clean the kitchen like you can, but they are learning. And along with the learning, they are feeling a sense of belonging to the family and building pride in their home.

There is another point I feel strongly about concerning this subject. Laziness has no place in the life of a Christian. If I allow my house to go unattended, to become dirty and totally cluttered because I am watching TV, catching up on social media, reading a book, talking aimlessly on the phone, or any other unnecessary "time grabber" activity, then I am doing wrong. None of these things are wrong in and of themselves, but when we don't use our time wisely and then make statements like, "I just don't have time to keep everything done in this house," we also are doing wrong.

The teachings of Jesus apply here, specifically the parable of the talents. That one-talent man buried what he had been given and was called a wicked and slothful (lazy) servant (Matt. 25:26). He didn't use his time to make what he had better. He only made excuses for why he hadn't done anything!

Do you find yourself using your children as an excuse for why the house is a wreck or the laundry isn't done? Do you ever say, "We can't have people over because the house is a mess"? Honestly examine yourself. Determine how to use your time wisely and enlist the help of everyone else in the household to keep things in order—not spotless, not uncomfortable, not untouchable—just in order. The benefits will bless not only you, but your family also.

If you haven't skipped over this section of the chapter, please understand that I realize there will be times when you are so busy that the housekeeping will have to be put on the back burner. Between doing good things for others and helping your husband with his ministry, household chores will be ignored. My advice to you is this: don't leave it there long. Get busy, enlist the help of your family, get out the Windex, and shine up that glass house!

A SHELTER FROM THE STORM

Life is often a storm for the preacher and his family. It can be relentless as a tidal wave of troubles and sorrows comes our way. I often quietly sing, "When the storms of life are raging, stand by me." Even though I may not know all of the troubles my husband is dealing with (because he so graciously protects me),

I can still see the concerns on his face.

In times like these, it is important to have a refuge. You need a place where you feel surrounded by love, a place of comfort, a place where you can occasionally close out everything else in order to relax and have some alone time. Your children also need this time alone with their parents. They need to learn that their home is a place of refuge and healing. Several years ago at a retreat, I heard a woman say "home" is the first hospital. She was making exactly the same point I am trying to make here.

When something hurtful, mean-spirited, or burdensome comes your way, what is the first thought that comes to your mind? For me, it's, "Where's Jim?" My husband is the first person that comes to my mind. I need to talk to him and cry on his shoulder, to be held and comforted by him. Our homes should be the first place our husbands and children think of when they need a shelter in the midst of the storms of life. It's not because of the physical structure, but because that's where people love and help you with whatever problem you may have.

LIVING IN A GLASS HOUSE IS TEMPORARY

I've been living in a glass house for 36 years now and, at times, I wonder how we made it this far. Our children are grown with families of their own, living in their own glass houses. Each day, I'm beginning to realize more clearly that I won't always be living in a glass house.

We used to have an elder's wife who would say something whenever anything negative happened: "This too shall pass." She was so right. Whatever we encounter in this earthly life is temporary. Those things we see and encounter on a daily basis are temporary. Those things that cause us grief are temporary.

Those things we spend so much time trying to accumulate are temporary. Those things we spend our valuable time worrying about are temporary.

My admonition to you is to enjoy living in your glass house and live your life to the fullest. You are visible, so set an example for others of how Jesus wants us to live.

EVERYONE LIVES IN A GLASS HOUSE

While you may struggle at times with the visibility of you and your family before others, let me leave you with what I consider to be a very uplifting passage from the writer of Hebrews. He is discussing rest for the people of God and makes this statement in 4:13: "And no creature is hidden from his [God's] sight, but all are naked and exposed to the eyes of him to whom we must give account."

We are not alone when it comes to living in a glass house. Let each one of us who has the privilege of serving God in the role of a preacher's wife become determined to set an example for others. Let us show them the joy that can only be found in serving God. Let them see us through our glass walls as we follow the teachings of Christ.

2

MAKING FRIENDS
Kathy Pollard

No doubt about it, the life of a minister's wife can be a lonely one.

- Your husband is basically on call 24/7. The time-consuming demands placed on him can make you feel like you're only getting the leftover scraps.

- You may have moved far away from your parents, siblings, and dear friends.

- Perhaps the title "preacher's wife" seems to have erected a barrier between you and any potential close friends.

- Maybe it seems like there are too many obstacles to having close friends.

- Or maybe you've been taught that you shouldn't have close friends.

For one or more of the above reasons, you may feel isolated even when surrounded by Christians. Yes, the life of a minister's wife can be a lonely one. But it doesn't have to be. This is strictly a matter of opinion, but I believe the preacher's wife can indeed have close friends. The wisdom literature in the Bible has too much to say about the subject for it to be something off-limits for certain people.

BLESSINGS OF HAVING CLOSE FRIENDS

Good friends offer strength. There will be times in your ministry when you feel discouraged, when you will stumble, or when you will feel weak. Solomon writes about strength in numbers. "Two are better than one, because they have a good reward for their toil. For if they fall, one will lift up his fellow. But woe to him who is alone when he falls and has not another to lift him up! Again, if two lie together, they keep warm, but how can one keep warm alone? And though a man might prevail against one who is alone, two will withstand him—a threefold cord is not quickly broken" (Eccl. 4:9-12).

Good friends offer advice. Everyone needs advice at some point, and the Bible has much to say about the counsel that comes from a trusted friend. "Oil and perfume make the heart glad, and the sweetness of a friend comes from his earnest counsel" (Prov. 27:9). "Iron sharpens iron, and one man sharpens another" (Prov. 27:17).

Good friends offer love. "A friend loves at all times" (Prov. 17:17a). Yes, you have a whole congregation of brothers and sisters who love you, but there's something special about the friends who know your hopes and what matters to you. Good friends have seen you in moments of low self-esteem. They know more of your hidden cares. And they love you for your own sake. C. S. Lewis once said, "Friendship is unnecessary, like philosophy, like art...It has no survival value; rather it is one of those things which gives value to survival."

HOW TO MAKE FRIENDS

More than one preacher's wife has struggled with making friends. Some feel that when they're introduced as "the preacher's wife," it's the kiss of death. They say it changes how the other person responds. The other person begins to act more reserved in their presence. They miss the depth and warmth that comes when folks feel like they can be real around them. Some preachers' wives have even felt like they can only seek friends from the community where they're seen as just another dedicated mom or loyal customer.

Take heart, preacher's wife. It doesn't have to be that way. Shouldn't your closest friends be ones who share your same spiritual goals? "What draws people to be friends is that they see the same truth. They share it," C. S. Lewis writes. With a little thought, your sisters in Christ can also be your true friends.

Be warm and approachable. This may seem like a no-brainer, but how you come across will certainly affect how well you make friends. You can probably think of someone you know whom your first impression of wasn't that great. Perhaps you thought they were cold and standoffish. After getting to know them, however, you learned that was far from the case. It took some time, but you found they had a heart of gold. What kind of first impression do you imagine you make? When someone meets you, not knowing your story or your personality, what do they instantly read about you? It needs to be that you are warm and friendly. It's that simple.

For introverts, being warm and approachable will take more

effort. You'll need to smile more and make your eyes light up when you greet others. You'll need to walk up to others and initiate the conversation. When I was a teenager, my dad kept reminding me to smile. He said I looked stuck up when I wasn't smiling. I wasn't stuck up at all; I was just shy. My dad helped me see that I needed to make a concerted effort to smile more so I would appear more warm and friendly. If it's painfully difficult for you to reach out, pray about it. God knows the desires of your heart. Ask him to help you think more of others by offering them cheery warmth.

Assume everyone likes you. And really, why wouldn't they? If you are kind, honest, and compassionate, then you are going to be a great friend to have. Give everyone the benefit of the doubt. Assume they are bright enough to see you for who you are. Don't make others prove their genuine intentions. Take their words at face value. Don't assume they're just being polite.

Sometimes we classify people and make false assumptions based on those categories. "She probably won't want to be friends with me. She's too _____ (e.g. "pretty," "young," "wealthy," "outgoing," etc.)." Don't rob others of your friendship because you're intimidated by their looks, status, or personality. Instead, assume they're going to like you and offer them your friendliest grin.

Be yourself. God made you uniquely you. Be thankful for that and glorify him by not hiding your special traits. If you imagine there is a certain persona you're supposed to carry, you're mistaken. Yes, the preacher's wife should be morally upright, humble, forgiving, friendly, and loving, but so should every Christian woman. Marrying a preacher doesn't mean you can't be you. Your husband chose you to be his wife. There must be something pretty special about you. Don't change! Don't hide your sense of humor! If your laugh sounds like a donkey, laugh anyway. People will be drawn to you because you are comfortable in your own skin.

Some preachers' wives have gone to extremes to prove that they're not going to be forced into some stifling role. They don't want the church to expect them to be the typical preacher's wife, so they go out of their way to shock the members with antics or brusque personality. It's almost as if they do all they can to make the congregation uncomfortable in order to force a confrontation about what it means to be a preacher's wife. This is not the kind of being real I'm talking about. If you love the bride of Christ, you will do all you can to promote harmony and respect the feelings of others. As the saying goes, "Be yourself, but be your best self."

Be open about your needs. It's okay to talk about what you'd like to accomplish as a preacher's wife. For instance, your friends will need to understand that you'd like to use the time before and after worship to meet visitors and greet other members (more about that later). They'll also need to understand that you can't be their source of information concerning sensitive issues or leadership matters. You may be privy to information that needs to be kept quiet. You're going to need friends who won't take that personally, and who won't feel miffed when you can't spend all of your time with them.

Don't be sensitive about your title. I know being introduced as "the preacher's wife" really bothers some. They feel like they've lost their identity or something. They silently seethe, "I have a name. " It has never bothered me. After all, I'm in love with the preacher. When people introduce you that way, they want their friends, guests, and family members to know who you are. Their guests already know who the preacher is because his role is such a visible one. They probably just want to help their guests connect the dots and put the two of you together. I think it's a good thing. After all, if they were ashamed of you, they would go out of their way not to introduce you as the preacher's wife.

Renita Archey is a warm and loving preacher's wife in Tennessee. These are her thoughts about being introduced as a preacher's wife:

> Most people call themselves "Christians," but because they call me "the preacher's wife," many times co-workers come to me with Bible questions or with an issue in their life where they need help. I don't believe I would be able to have as many Bible studies over lunch without that title. Right now, two ladies that I work with are attending my ladies' class at the Chattanooga School of Preaching and Biblical Studies. It opened the door to an in-depth study on the role of women leaders in the church. Another co-worker approached me when her daughter came home talking about 'a young earth.' She had never heard the term before, and we studied for several weeks. I also cannot remember the number of times two of us have retreated to the restroom for a session of prayer over a specific issue they were facing.

If you are one who resents being introduced as "the preacher's wife," try to keep those feelings hidden (at least during that introduction). Raising your eyebrows or making a remark only makes the one you're being introduced to feel uncomfortable. You'll just need to get over yourself for a bit. Instead of focusing on the title, focus on the opportunity to offer warmth and a smile to the person you're meeting.

Open your heart. You might get hurt, it's true. The church is made up of imperfect humans. Someone might say something thoughtless or unkind. They might neglect your friendship or even abuse your trust. But don't erect a barrier to protect your heart. That's no way to live. Keeping people at arm's length will only make you feel lonely.

Maybe you're wondering what it really means to open your heart, practically speaking. One idea is to look up all the "one another" passages in the New Testament. Write down the ways God tells us to interact with one another. For example, we're to:

- "love one another" (John 13:34-35)

- "be devoted to one another" (Rom. 12:10)

- "honor one another above yourselves" (Rom. 12:10)

- "accept one another" (Rom. 15:7)

- "greet one another" (Rom. 16:16)

- "serve one another" (Gal. 5:13)

- "bear with one another" (Eph. 4:2)

- "submit to one another" (Eph. 5:21)

These are just a few of the many "one another" passages. If you make an effort to practice these things, then you will know that you are opening your heart.

Get the chip off your shoulder. Maybe you met someone and just didn't hit it off. Your personalities clashed, or you felt her disdain or indifference. Please don't assume it must be because you're the preacher's wife. Everyone has had similar experiences, preacher's wife or not. All you need to worry about is making sure you're offering sincere warmth. If that warmth is not returned, try not to take it personally.

These tips for making friends are just reminders to make sure you are doing your part in reaching out. You don't want to be guilty of complaining of not having any friends if you haven't done all you can to be friendly. C. S. Lewis reminds us, "Friendship is not a reward for our discriminating and good taste in finding one another out. It is the instrument by which God reveals to each of us the beauties of others."

WHAT IF THERE'S NO FRIEND IN SIGHT?

If you worship with a small congregation, you may discover there aren't many options. It may be a friendly church, but you don't have any close friends. There are some things you can do when you find yourself without good friends.

Give it more time. Friendships don't happen overnight. It could be that some event or activity in the future will help you form a bond with another woman. About a year after my husband and I moved to Colorado, we went on a short-term mission trip to Tanzania with a few other Christians from our congregation. Lynn was one of the ladies who traveled with us. Before the trip, Lynn and I were on friendly terms, but not the least bit close. We came home from the trip with great experiences and a new relationship. We've been close friends ever since. If you've only been with a congregation for a year or two, be patient.

Think outside the box. You might envision a certain type of woman as a close friend, but there may be potential friends in other age groups that you haven't considered. Even though you may not have as many common interests as women your own age, you can still learn from and enjoy friendships with women in a different time of life. You may be surprised to find that some of your dearest friends could be a decade or more older or younger than you.

Reach out to other preachers' wives. If you're searching for a friend who just "gets it," try attending one of the retreats for preachers' wives. You'll probably make some life-long friends, in addition to finding spiritual renewal and refreshment. Also, take advantage of the Facebook groups for ministers' wives (avoid the ones that are mostly gripe sessions).

Trust God. It could be that this is just a time in your life when you'll need to rely on the dear companions you already have (your husband and your Savior). Don't let a lack of close friends keep you from being happy and content.

SOME CONSIDERATIONS

While I believe preachers' wives can have close friends, I also believe that wisdom must be used in those friendships. You could unknowingly hurt your ministry if you neglect to consider a few things.

Choose your friends carefully. Some women wouldn't be a good influence over you. For instance, avoid becoming close friends with a gossip, one who isn't discreet, or one who lacks self-control. The Scriptures warn us that spending time with these types of folks will rub off on us:

- "Make no friendship with a man given to anger, nor go with a wrathful man, lest you learn his ways and entangle yourself in a snare" (Prov. 22:24-25).

- "Whoever walks with the wise becomes wise, but the companion of fools will suffer harm" (Prov. 13:20).

- "Do not be deceived: 'Bad company ruins good morals'" (1 Cor. 15:33).

Protect confidences. It's wonderful to spend time with a good friend over a cup of coffee. If you have a very good friend, you're probably comfortable sharing your thoughts and feelings with her. What a blessing! But as was mentioned earlier, sometimes you'll be aware of things that should be kept confidential. Guard against the need to share everything with your dear friend. Resist the desire to want to seem "in the know" by dropping hints or divulging information. There's never a good reason to betray a confidence. It only takes one occasion of loose lips to destroy trust.

Protect your husband. Sometimes women just want to be able to gripe about their husband's lapse of judgment or his thoughtless comment. Be very careful about sharing private things about your husband. Remember, he is also your friend's preacher. She will be seeing him in the pulpit each week and needs to be able to listen to the gospel without the baggage of knowing your latest gripe with him.

Use your time at the assemblies wisely. Being an introvert myself, I know how tempting it is to socialize only with close friends before and after worship services. It's easy and comfortable. But to do so would be to rob the other members of my encouragement (Heb. 10:24-25). You can set up other times during the week to visit with your good friends. You should focus on greeting visitors and growing your relationship with the other members while at the church building. You also don't want to appear cliquish by only hanging out with the same circle of friends each week. Make it your goal to converse with as many people as possible, and to share the same level of warmth with every member and visitor that you share with your good friends.

Don't resent your husband's job if you can't join every social activity. It could be that your family's income isn't as great as that of your friends. If they're always going out to eat, but you can't afford to join them every time, don't sulk about it. Don't feel like you are "missing out." And definitely don't start making comments like, "Must be nice..."

Don't let close friendships keep you from a move. Your husband may feel it's time to consider a move. He may want to accept a job offer in a new location. Naturally, it would be hard to leave your close friends, but that's not a good enough reason to object to the move. Your husband needs to work where he feels he can accomplish the most good.

Don't let your friends become the focus of your work. Your primary job is outreach and hospitality. If your closest friends are the only ones you're having into your home, you've let them become the focus of your work. It's okay to have them over as often as you like, but try inviting the elderly, members you don't know as well, or visitors over at the same time.

When you get involved in a project like VBS or Bible camp, are your closest friends the ones you ask for help? If so, you need to broaden your list of recruits. You can encourage a young, new member by asking her to be your VBS co-teacher or Bible camp co-counselor. Or ask someone that you think doesn't even like you to go visiting with you or help you provide a meal for someone. Of course, I'm not saying you can't ever work together with your best friends. Just make sure that you also include many others in those great works.

These considerations might seem unfair, but they aren't really. In fact, they are considerations that every Christian woman should make, not just the preacher's wife.

Can a preacher's wife have close friends? I believe so. With a little wisdom and a lot of warmth, you can enjoy a special bond of friendship with those whom God has placed in your life.

3

SUPPORTING YOUR HUSBAND
Lea Morgan

efore my husband, Trey, and I married, he was already preparing for the ministry. When he was a twenty-year-old college student, he took a job as a church's youth minister in a small town about an hour from home. He would travel there every weekend, hang out with the teens, plan youth activities and devotionals, as well as teach the Sunday morning teen Bible class. The minister of the church was a great mentor for Trey, teaching him what to do and what not to do in his ministry. One Sunday evening, he gave Trey the opportunity to preach. Trey had never preached a sermon before, but he is not one to back down from a challenge. Trey gladly welcomed the opportunity.

When the day finally arrived, Trey's dad proudly made the hour-long drive to hear his son preach his first sermon. Trey nervously stumbled through his lesson, knowing he was making several blunders. He had picked out a song that went perfectly with the lesson and, before he concluded the lesson, he asked the congregation to sing along with him. As he got a couple of lines into the song, he realized he was singing a solo because no one knew the song! Needless to say, he only sang one verse and then quickly wrapped up his lesson.

He was embarrassed and humiliated because he felt like he had not done a very good job. He decided right then and there that the first sermon he ever preached would also be his last. He never wanted to do that again. So when he made his way to the back of the auditorium, he dreaded every second of it because he would have to face all the members as they left the building. A few of them shook his hand and gave him an obligatory "good job" or "great lesson." He thanked them, but knew they were only being kind.

One of the last people to make his way to the back of the auditorium was Trey's dad. Trey wondered if he had embarrassed him, but then something happened that changed everything. Trey's dad shook his son's hand and said, "That was the best lesson I have ever heard. Don't ever stop preaching."

You see, my future husband was feeling broken and discouraged. He was ready to throw in the towel and quit, but the support from his father that night made all the difference in the world. He was encouraged to keep preaching, and that was what he needed. He could have easily made the decision that ministry really wasn't for him, but with the support of his godly parents, he decided to enroll in the Sunset School of Preaching to continue his training. Almost thirty years later, he is still going strong, doing what he loves best.

Since Trey was already training for ministry before we married, being a minister's wife is all I have ever known. I gladly took on the role of supporter that is so vital in ministry.

WHY IS SUPPORT SO VITAL TO MINISTRY?

The world is full of critics and, unfortunately, ministers get their fair share of criticism. When it comes to lessons, the English majors are quick to point out all the grammatical errors and mispronounced words. If there is a PowerPoint, the misspelled words will be glaringly obvious. The Bible scholars will certainly take issue with the way a verse is translated or misquoted. If a minister accidentally says Jonah (instead of Joshua) marched around the wall seven times, he will certainly hear about it.

Nothing your husband does will please every single person, and there will always be someone who is eager to suggest a better way of doing things. One person might think the minister needs to be in the office studying more, while another person suggests that he needs to be out making more visits and reaching out to the community. A minister is constantly being pulled in different directions by the opinions of members, as well as leadership. He desperately needs to know that someone is in his corner. He especially needs to know that his wife is his biggest fan and cheerleader.

If a minister does not have the support of his wife, the ministry will fail, the marriage will fail, or both. So how can a minister's wife fully support her husband? There are four ways a wife can bless her husband in his ministry. She can support him spiritually, physically, emotionally, and verbally.

SPIRITUAL SUPPORT

James 5:16 tells us, "The prayer of a righteous person has great power as it is working." Prayer is a powerful and effective way for a wife to support her husband. Ask God to help you pray for your husband daily. Ask your husband what you can pray for on his behalf. The Bible provides help in this matter.

- Pray that he lives in accordance with God's plan for his life, which includes being humble, gentle, and patient (Eph. 4:1-2).

- Pray that God will be glorified in your marriage (Eph. 5:25-33).

- Pray that the Lord will bless his work (Prov. 22:29, Col. 3:23-24).

- Pray that he will be a man of integrity (Prov. 11:3).

- Pray that he will be guarded from temptation (1 Cor. 10:13).

- Pray for his discernment in handling finances (Luke 16:13).

- Pray that he would seek wisdom (Jas. 1:5).

- Pray for his health (3 John 2).

- Pray that the Lord will give him strength (Psa. 28:7).

- Pray that he would be surrounded by people who build him up (Prov. 13:20).

- Pray that he would boldly declare the truth of the gospel (Acts 28:31).

- Pray that he would continue to grow spiritually through reading, studying, and prayer (2 Pet. 3:18).

- Pray that he would have a humble, teachable spirit (Prov. 15:33).

- Pray that he would be full of patience and peace (Rom. 14:19).

- Pray that he would be quick to forgive (Eph. 4:32).

Praying for your husband will not only mold his heart to look more like Jesus', but it changes you from the inside out. I grow more in love with my husband the more I pray for him. My husband and I are two imperfect people, in love with each other and in love with Jesus. As I pray for my husband, I pray all the more that God will mold me into the wife and woman of God he has made me to be. Lift your husband up to God. He needs your spiritual support through prayer.

PHYSICAL SUPPORT

I am a detail-oriented person. I am good with numbers, planning, and organizing. On the other hand, I don't show a lot of enthusiasm, and I'm not very comfortable in front of a crowd. Trey is a people-person. He thrives on being with people, young and old. He is very expressive and is a great public speaker. However, details bore him, and he is not the best event organizer. When it comes to Trey and I, the expression "opposites attract" hits the nail right on the head. His strengths are my weaknesses, and my strengths are his weaknesses. This works to our advantage when it comes to doing ministry together.

Trey has a wonderful vision in ministry, but sometimes needs a little help putting his plan together. This is where I am able to offer support physically by working alongside him to help him achieve his goals.

For instance, since we have always worked with churches in small towns, we have not been blessed with an education minister. Thus, the daunting task of planning Vacation Bible School has fallen to the minister. Trey does a lot of things well, but he would be the first person to tell you that planning a VBS from start to finish is not one of them. He is great at writing drama and puppet skits and coming up with fun ideas, but he wouldn't have a clue where to start with the organization of it all. I, however, do not blink an eye at the thought of making learning center rotation schedules, time schedules, sign up sheets, etc. He is great at enlisting volunteers, building excitement, and being the front man for VBS. This is teamwork at its best! We combine our efforts to reach a common goal. My support in organizing and planning is essential to my husband, and I have no doubt that the physical support you offer is essential to your husband as well.

The saying, "Behind every great or successful man there stands a woman," is true in this instance. It emphasizes that the success of a man is often determined by the work and support of his wife. We succeed when our men succeed, so let's physically offer our support by working right alongside them.

EMOTIONAL SUPPORT

A great wife is there to listen to her husband and help him deal with various issues that arise. She offers emotional support, which makes her husband feel better about himself. Did you know that Laura Bush helped persuade her husband to stop drinking when he was in his early forties? She was an emotional rock when her husband needed it the most. Thanks to Laura's emotional strength, George W. Bush went on to become the Governor of Texas and the President of the United States. The sky is the limit for what your husband can accomplish by having a loving, supportive wife who will refuel his emotional tank when necessary.

An emotionally supportive wife also allows her husband to take risks. Taking risks involves faith, and Jesus did not call us to serve others from the comfort of our recliners. Ministry involves taking risks. Share your husband's dreams and allow him to step out in faith and take the required risks. Napoleon Bonaparte is renowned as one of the greatest military minds in history. He married Josephine in March 1796 just before he marched off to conquer Italy on behalf of France. In letters, he gives credit to his wife for fueling his confidence to accomplish this feat.

Ministry is filled with highs and lows, and each high and low carries significant emotional swings. An emotionally supportive wife will allow her husband to reach for the stars, but be there to catch him if he falls. A life of ministry can easily wear your husband down, but remember the church you both serve is Jesus' church. There will be people that disappoint you and possibly even hurt you or your husband's ministry. Always remember to love the church, because it is Christ's church, not ours. We serve Christ above all.

VERBAL SUPPORT

By praising your husband and not demeaning his ideas and vision, a supportive wife strokes her husband's ego and gives him the confidence he needs to be a great minister. Ask God to remind you frequently of the importance of your words! The chances are great that the self-esteem of your husband rises and falls with your words. Proverbs 18:21 tells us, "Death and life are in the power of the tongue."

Pointing out all of your husband's flaws will only deflate and discourage him. Hold your tongue and only point out mistakes when it is constructive and truly helpful. For example, if he mispronounces a word four times in the same sermon, it is okay to gently break the news to him so he won't do it again. Otherwise, he needs to hear that you think that was the best sermon he has ever preached. Be his biggest cheerleader. Only positive feedback can motivate people to continue doing what they're doing.

Why do you think men have a hard time "cutting the apron strings" from their mothers? Mothers praise their children from the time they are born. Every little accomplishment becomes the greatest, most amazing thing in the world! They are praised when they say their first word. They are praised when they begin to crawl. They are praised when they walk, pick a flower and bring it to her, draw a picture, write their name, hit a ball, and on and on it goes for their entire life. It doesn't stop when they are grown. A mother still thinks her son is the best thing since sliced bread, and she probably tells him often. A wife needs to praise her husband more than his mother does. You don't want anyone to praise your husband more than you do, even his mother, so be the president of his fan club, so to speak.

One time, my oldest son, Taylor, was about five and asked his daddy if they could go play catch. Trey was willing, but Taylor had specific instructions for this session of catch. He said, "Dad, you are going to throw me the ball, and when I catch it, you're going to say 'good job.'" You see, part of what Taylor enjoyed so much about playing catch with his dad was the praise he knew he was going to receive. When it comes to needing praise, your husband is just a little boy in a grown-up's body. He will never grow out of needing verbal support, praise, and encouragement.

We all respond better to praise and encouragement than we do criticism. You have heard the saying that it takes five positive comments to make up for one criticism. According to relationship researcher John Gottman, marriages fall into the danger zone of divorce when the ratio of positive to negative interactions falls below the five-to-one ratio. Scientists have found that this ratio can be used to predict everything from workplace performance to divorce. Not only is verbal support important to your husband as a minister, it is important to your marriage as well. Let your husband know what you appreciate about him and do it often. Thank him for what he does for you. Compliment him. Respect him always.

Recently, Trey agreed to help some good friends of ours, Paul and Stacey, build a new fence for their backyard. The old, dilapidated pickets were torn down, and brand new pickets began going up in their place. After they got several feet of fence built, Stacey came out of the house to check on their progress. After she inspected it for a minute, she asked, "Why is it a little crooked?" Paul and Trey explained that one section was not going to be perfectly straight because the original metal post that was cemented into the ground was not completely level, but they assured her it would not be noticeable once the entire fence was up. She then questioned something else about the fence. Trey responded with a smile on his face, "Here is what we need you to do: About every twenty to thirty minutes, we need you to come out of the house and tell us how great the fence looks and what a good job we are doing." She asked, "Why do I need to do that?" Trey responded, "Because it will makes us work better, harder, and faster, and you will love the results."

Stacey agreed to the challenge, and sure enough, every few minutes she would stick her head out the door and say, "You guys are doing an awesome job!" and "That is a great looking fence," and "Y'all are working hard!" After a while, she had to go to work, but not too long after she had gone, Trey and Paul both received text messages that said, "I can't see the fence, but I know it looks great!" They had a lot of laughs and it made the work seem less tedious. What a difference praise can make!

I believe Eph. 4:29 should be every wife's mission when it comes to her husband. The NLT reads, "Don't use foul or abusive language. Let everything you say be good and helpful, so that your words will be an encouragement to those who hear them." The NIV puts it this way: "Do not let any unwholesome talk come out of your mouths, but only what is helpful for building others up according to their needs, that it may benefit those who listen." The Message paraphrases Eph. 4:29 in this way: "Watch the way you talk. ... Say only what helps, each word a gift."

The words Trey's father spoke to him after that first failed sermon were a gift. Those words encouraged Trey to keep preaching, even when he felt like he had messed up royally. There will be days in ministry when your husband feels like he has messed up royally, too. Let your words always be gifts to your husband. Support him spiritually through prayer. Support him physically with help. Support him emotionally by being a sounding board. Support him verbally with praise.

4

BEING A SINGLE MOM IN THE PEW
Melanie Jenkins

"Train up a child in the way he should go; even when he is old he will not depart from it" (Prov. 22:6).

Now to be clear, I'm not bitter or angry at all. But for all practical purposes, I was a single mom in the pew at every church service. While my husband was standing before the audience telling people how to train their children, I was training his— uhhh, ours. While he fulfilled the Lord's need for one to preach that they might hear (Rom. 10:14-15), I was quietly preaching my own sermons to two precious souls who occupied the pew with me. Now, every mom has sacrifices to make. But in the congregation, mine were exceptionally unique. My life is richer for these sacrifices, and I believe my husband's ministry is more effective because of them.

Sacrifice does not always mean suffering, and the fruit of these sacrifices has been so sweet to enjoy. It has yielded two sons in effective ministry who love the Lord, two daughters-in-law who seem the perfect match for our sons, and a host of other joys not excluding the simple satisfaction of seeing my greatest desire come to pass—to rear children to love and obey God. Every parent can relate to 3 John 4, "I have no greater joy than to hear that my children are walking in the truth."

From the first moment I knew I was having a child, my prayer life grew like the hearts of all mothers do! Prayers for health, safety, wise choices, their future spouse, that we wouldn't mess them up for God, but instead would return them to him. One could easily go from unbridled joy to abject terror on those thoughts alone. While this is an awesome task, it need not be a joyless, trembling one. Rearing our children is a huge responsibility, one to be approached on our knees and with a heart full of joy and love to teach them daily about worshiping the Lord.

These children are yours—love them—but also remember to train them. "These words that I command you today shall be on your heart. You shall teach them diligently to your children, and shall talk of them when you sit in your house, and when you walk by the way, and when you lie down, and when you rise" (Deut. 6:6-7). While written to the children of Israel, modern Israel (the church) should still remember these words.

We have been blessed with two sons who love the Lord, who selected spouses who are faithful Christians and are a great fit for their lives. I thank God that they are both faithful ministers, and that they love him with all their heart, soul, mind, and strength.

When I hear them pray, preach, or read what they write, I am overwhelmed at what God does through them and feel blessed that he allowed me to be a partner with my husband and the other influences in their lives to help them become the godly men they now are. Humbly, I want to emphasize that I could not have done this without the blessings of God and the support of my husband. The experience has also been made much sweeter by friends and leaders who have cared for our family.

People want to know how we did it. To be honest, I'm not sure, and I'd want to avoid a list looking like we had it all together or that this is a pattern for success. Just as every child is different, every family is different, and you need to find what works and doesn't work when it comes to meeting the spiritual needs of your children. Let your children be children, and let them grow with your love and kindness. Our children are not perfect, nor are their parents. All children desire a childhood of sweet memories, and a large part of those memories will be things they learn at your side in the pew.

That said, here is some of what we believe worked for us:

1. WE EXPECTED OUR CHILDREN TO LIVE AND DO RIGHT

While we have never been even close to perfect, we also tried to live the lives in the privacy of our home that we claimed in public. How hypocritical it would be to teach a life of purity, yet use acid words toward our family members. How sinful to speak with love in the "church house" about the church, but belittle brothers and sisters in our own house. How sad it would be to encourage joyful Christian living before the watching masses, but to live lives of unhappiness before our little family. It was a given in our home that we were going to strive to live the Lord's way at all times and in every setting. This is not a game—it is a war against the enemy.

2. THE WORK YOU DO IS MINISTRY

At this point, raising your children is your most important ministry. Sisters, while we are by name and nature to be servants (imitating the Great Servant), do not be so busy yourself with church work that you forget you are commanded directly by God to be a keeper at home, to direct your home (Tit. 2:4-5). If you lead every women's ministry and have your hand in every project at church, you'll be a hero to everyone except those you are most responsible for—your own children. If you lead the whole community to Christ and not your own children, peaceful joy will be hard to find. So don't feel guilty that you can't do everything at church. You have your ministry. But also don't use your children as an excuse not to be active in the work of the church in some way. If you are not involved, your husband's ministry will suffer, your spiritual life will suffer, and your example to your children will teach them it's okay not to be active in the work of the church.

3. PRAY

Your mission is really the same as Hannah's pledge, to give your children back to the Father. Paul says to "be constant in prayer" (Rom. 12:12). The word translated "constant" is only used here and in Eph. 6:18. Why are we so strongly encouraged to be constant, faithful, and persistent in something so obvious? Probably because it is very easy for us to get so busy, even in good things, that we miss this best thing. Surrounded by crying babies and smelly diapers, overwhelmed with life and laundry, prayer could get pushed to the fringes. Remember to solicit your greatest Ally in your most grand attempt—God himself. Pray for your children's safety, their future spouses, their friendships, their future work, and for their faith. Pray that you'll know how to answer their deepest questions, that they'll run to your side when they are hurting, and that you'll know when they are going astray. Pray as you go about your day. Pray as you drive them to their various activities. Pray when you rock them. Pray for and *with* them. By your example, you are teaching them the importance of depending on God in prayer. Pray.

4. EXPECT THEM TO BEHAVE

Children are going to push the boundaries. From the youngest of ages, expect them to behave. Yes, children will be children. They will not be the perfect little angels that your church directory or Christmas card depicts, and you should let them have great fun. But that fun does not need to be rooted in sin. I remember hearing a parenting expert years ago saying that children *want* and need boundaries. Teach that we do right in this family, not because dad's a preacher or there is a paycheck involved, but because right is right. What is good behavior in the pew to you? While some things are relative, some are not. Be careful not to allow someone else's definition of "behavior" to bring frustration into the training of your children. Children can learn to respect the time of worship. Teach them to sit and work quietly, to fold their hands in prayer, and to sing along with their sweet voices. Every Christian around them will be edified.

5. SPEAK HIGHLY OF THE CHURCH AND ITS LEADERS

No elder or eldership is perfect, and some will be more challenging to work under than others. But their imperfections do not delete the Spirit's imperatives: "We ask you, brothers, to respect those who labor among you and are over you in the Lord and admonish you, and to esteem them very highly in love because of their work. Be at peace among yourselves" (1

Thess. 5:12-13). When an eldership disappoints you because of a decision, disagreement, or deed, it becomes easy to let your disappointment spiral out of control and lead to disrespect. But remember, your children know what a hypocrite is even if they can't spell it. If you fain respect in public, but speak ill of them in private, it will affect their future faith adversely. If you bad-mouth them at home, but still take a paycheck they endorse, you are sending a mixed message. Be careful with your words, or your children will grow up troubled and suspicious of God's leaders.

Don't lie to make a poor leader look good. Instead, teach your children about how we are all sinners, even the best of leaders, and that sin hurts people, but that we are all growing and learning and trying to please God as his family. It is almost as dangerous never to discuss mistakes and disagreements as it is to hone in on them all the time. Let them see that elders are real people who are in this struggle against evil *with* us. This is also an opportunity to teach them about forgiveness.

6. DEVELOP A SURROGATE FAMILY IN THE CHURCH

What would we do without friends? Seek out fun, godly people who are older than you and can be surrogate grandparents to your children. In ministry, it will be rare that you will live close to grandparents. Church grandparents people will love your children and will help you be a better parent if you let them. They have already raised their children and can share insights that will aid you. Find people who are your same parenting age whom you can enjoy the journey with and share in the challenges and joy.

7. BE AN EXAMPLE TO OTHERS

The best thing we can be is a good example: both those who went before us, as well as their written accounts are examples (Heb. 12:1; 1 Cor. 10:10-11). Older women are to be an example of faith to younger women and older men to younger men (Tit. 2). The young are to be an example (1 Tim. 4:12), and elders are to be an example to the flock (1 Pet. 5:3). We are to be an example in how we deal with our struggles (1 Pet. 2:21). Our congregations are commanded to be examples to each other (1 Thess. 1:7). We are all to be examples to each other (Phil. 3:17). Even Jesus himself did things as an example (John 13:15). As a Christian mother (more than just a preacher's wife), you need to be a good example to those around you. Share with your fellow laborers so they might learn and grow, and you will grow as well. We are never in this alone—we have Jesus' word on that (Matt. 28:20).

8. DISCIPLINE

"Don't fail to discipline your children. The rod of punishment won't kill them. Physical discipline may well save them from death" (Prov. 23:13-14 NLT). The younger you start training your children to obey, the easier it will be as they grow older. Also, remember that different children respond to discipline in different ways. Some need only a look, others just a word, and some need more corporal inducement. Be consistent in your discipline. Sometimes, preachers' families are hurt by the brethren. In that hurt, it may be tempting to become permissive as parents to try to make that pain less painful. Our pain does not minimize the significance of the Scriptures or change it.

When it comes to discipline, we also need to remember not to exasperate our children with too many rules (Eph. 6:4).

9. MAKE WORSHIP SOMETHING TO LOOK FORWARD TO

Help your children learn to enjoy the time of worship with others. Learn members' names. Don't isolate your children; introduce your children to them and tell them something special about that person. Seek out those members who might need a smile and/or a hug from your child. These may last a lifetime and will teach your children to appreciate others in God's family all of their lives and wherever they go. Remember Psa. 122:1, "I was glad when they said to me, 'Let us go to the house of the Lord!'"

10. BUILD MARGIN TO AVOID ALWAYS BEING LATE

If every Sunday is a mad dash to the door, it will sap some of the joy and peace from your worship. Sometimes it may be that you are the only one home to get everybody dressed, ready, in the car, and on the way. Plan ahead.

11. GIVE YOUR CHILDREN FREEDOM TO ASK ANYTHING

Our children are going to ask questions. How we listen and respond will determine if they come back and ask more. Set the cooking aside, stop the ironing, put down the smartphone, and listen. Take time to hear and answer with a mother's heart. Don't over-react when they tell you something bad they did, or something horrible a friend did—if you do, they may not return when they need to share something in the future, and they will find another source or outlet for that information.

12. ENJOY YOURSELF & YOUR FAMILY

As a minister's family, you will not only enjoy the best moments of people's lives (births, baptisms, weddings), but you are also going to have to encounter a lot of other people's pain and deal with a lot of heavy stuff like souls and salvation. You are going to have to be there for people in their hardest and darkest moments—avoid dwelling there. The Bible says that eventually our tears will be taken away, but such is not said of our joy or our laughter. Don't take yourself too seriously, and don't forget that the same God who made emotions made them all, laughter included. So enjoy the journey! Laugh a lot. Make time for your family a priority. Be the best you that God has created you to be. Enjoy your husband and children that God has given you. You may never have a lot of money or stuff, but you will have a large collection of friends and memories, and I promise you it will never be boring.

Never forget that you are blessing the future more than you know. I thank God for your faith and service. Your impact is greater than you realize.

Be a blessing in and out of the pew. Some of those best memories will bring a smile to your face, a tear to the corner of your eye, a slight giggle, and a feeling of satisfaction as you recall those precious moments as a single mom in the pew.

5

HONORING CONFIDENTIALITY
Beverly Watkins

It was a few days before Christmas, and I was wrapping gifts. Rachel, our youngest daughter, was 2½ years old. She came into the room and asked me what I was doing.

Me: I'm wrapping your gift for Daddy.
Rachel: What is it?
Me: It's a surprise.
Rachel: I won't tell.
Me: No, you will have to wait because it is a surprise for Daddy for Christmas.
Rachel: I won't tell him.
Me: Okay. You got him undershirts.

As soon as the words left my mouth, Rachel took off out of the bedroom, down the hall, and down the stairs to her daddy. I am behind her, telling her not to tell him. As soon as she sees him, she blurts out, "I got you undershirts." She then turns around and says to me, "I won't tell him again." And she

.hat he now knew what she got him for

:acher, I am often asked if I would sit and
,ans listening to someone else talk. I listen
s out their heart and soul, hoping to find
.omfort, answers, or just a sounding board.
This pe.   .ting me to hear them with my head, as well
as with my hea. . They have to know that their secret/problem
is safe with me.

Trust is a very precious thing. It is easily given. But once broken, it's almost never earned back.

Do you remember the commercial, "I told two friends, who told two friends, who told two friends?" Soon the screen was filled with the faces of people who knew this one piece of information. Granted, this was a commercial for shampoo, but the same thing happens when you break confidence. Have you ever thought, "I can trust my best friend not to tell anyone," only to find out that she has told another of her friends, who also wouldn't tell anyone, but then told her best friend, and so on? Before long, everyone knows and, more often than not, someone is hurt along the way.

When I was in elementary school, we played a game called "Gossip." The teacher would whisper a "secret" in one student's ear, and then that student whispered the "secret" into the next student's ear, and so on until the last student had heard the "secret." By the time it reached the last student, the "secret" was so distorted, it didn't sound anything like the original. We would laugh at how different it had become, how nonsensical. This is exactly what happens to a confidence that is not kept. The original statement never sounds anything like the final one, and the problem is that it isn't funny; it's hurtful.

Proverbs 11:13 says, "Whoever goes about slandering

reveals secrets, but he who is trustworthy in spirit keeps a thing covered." All ministry and relationships are based on trust.

We trust our doctors with our most intimate health issues. We trust our attorneys with our last will and testament, as well as with the information required for our defense. We trust our accountants with the most private details about our income and liabilities. We trust our counselors with our childhood experiences, fears, relationships, and deepest secrets. We do this, not only because we believe they are capable, but also because we believe they will keep our confidences. In fact, we know it is illegal to disclose this information to others.

Have you noticed that the people in whom we have confidence are usually the same people with whom we will share a confidence? When a person has proven she is trustworthy, we are far more likely to trust her with our secrets, fears, hopes, and dreams. Don't expect someone to share their heart with you if they do not believe they can trust you. Keeping a confidence is about more than keeping a secret. It begins and ends with your character. People will come to you with their deepest thoughts, feelings, failures, and fears only when they know that those disclosures are safe and secure in your heart and hands. When that trust is broken, they become doubly damaged. By faithfully holding what people have revealed to you—by maintaining confidentiality—you can improve relationships and help people's personal healing.

When someone you know shares feelings or thoughts that are troubling her, or something that makes her feel guilty, it can be very tempting to share that information with someone else. Even when your motives are driven by kindness and concern (e.g. wanting to pass the information along as a prayer request), it could be damaging or painful to the person who first shared the information.

If you really believe something needs to be passed along (for prayer or to someone else whom you believe could help), tell that to the person who shared it with you. Explain to her why you believe others should know and encourage her to pass it along to the appropriate people. At the very least, get permission before you share any private information.

Confidentiality should be our standard at all times and in every relationship. It encourages trust, growth, and healing in the body of Christ. "There is one whose rash words are like sword thrusts, but the tongue of the wise brings healing" (Prov. 12:18). Here are other Scriptures that show God's interest in our honoring confidences:

- "A prudent man conceals knowledge, but the heart of fools proclaims folly" (Prov. 12:23).

- "A gossip betrays a confidence; so avoid anyone who talks too much" (Prov. 20:19 NIV).

- "Without wood a fire goes out; without a gossip a quarrel dies down ... The words of a gossip are like choice morsels; they go down to the inmost parts" (Prov. 26:20, 22 NIV).

Keeping confidences is not easy. Benjamin Franklin famously wrote, "Three may keep a secret, if two of them are dead." There are times when our lives become difficult because we know too much rather than too little. If you are trustworthy, you will be in many conversations where personal secrets, disappointments, failures, and traumas are shared by people who are lonely and hurting. These confidences are often revealed as part of a desperate search for understanding or grace, for forgiveness or wholeness. Has there ever been a true friend who doesn't carry the burdens of someone else's calamity, helplessness, dreams, disappointments, or sin?

Every person you know has a story, and that story isn't always pretty. Hidden behind smiling faces are often hearts filled with turmoil, fear, and alarming failures. When these very private and tender wounds are laid open to you, it is neither a casual nor ordinary conversation. It is a sacred trust.

When someone opens their heart to you in this way, it is a cry for help and understanding; they need to be valued even when they find very little value in themselves. Behind these risks is a profound trust in your ability to keep a confidence, to receive their heart and not betray it to others. It is faith in your capacity to guard their secret well. Nothing can be more devastating than for you to forget this fundamental basis of trust on which people open their lives to you.

Don't accept a secret if you are not willing to be trustworthy, and keep in mind that this trust may present you with extreme difficulties. Most secrets involve other people. How will you relate to someone who might be connected with what you have been told? Most people will have no idea what you have discovered; realizing that you know these things could potentially cause them pain or embarrassment.

Another difficulty is that a confidence is usually revealed by one person, making it almost impossible to ask others for their side of the story. It's difficult, as well as dangerous at times, to enter into a casual conversation with others to try to understand the whole story without revealing what has been told to you in confidence.

Additional difficulty arises when the revelation made in confidence is so serious that it demands some kind of action. This is further complicated if a request has been made for the information to remain just between the two of you. In such a situation, you find yourself in a terrible moral and ethical dilemma. What can you do with information that is confidential? What if someone will be terribly hurt or possibly endangered unless you share what you have learned? Such danger seems to put two absolute values in conflict with one another—the absolute demand of keeping a confidence vs. the absolute demand of protecting the innocent.

My advice? Pray, pray, and pray some more. Unless the situation is an absolute emergency, I would counsel against any immediate decision. Take the time to ask the Lord for wisdom. James said, "If any of you lacks wisdom, let him ask God, who gives generously to all without reproach, and it will be given him. But let him ask in faith, with no doubting, for the one who doubts is like a wave of the sea that is driven and tossed by the wind. For that person must not suppose that he will receive anything from the Lord; he is a double-minded man, unstable in all his ways" (Jas. 1:5-8).

I realize that there is immense tension when two great and true principles seem to be in conflict. For me, when the principle of keeping confidence is in direct danger of destroying the true principle of protection of the innocent, I will always decide in favor of protecting the innocent. God's greatest anger was kindled when people neglected or abused the most vulnerable in society. For example, "You shall not mistreat any widow or fatherless child. If you do mistreat them, and they cry out to me, I will surely hear their cry, and my wrath will burn, and I will kill you with the sword, and your wives shall become widows and your children fatherless" (Exod. 22:22-24).

Another example of this is found in Amos 2:6-7a: "For three transgressions of Israel, and for four, I will not revoke the punishment, because they sell the righteous for silver, and the needy for a pair of sandals— those who trample the head of the poor into the dust of the earth and turn aside the way of the afflicted." God pours out his wrath on those who do not protect the innocent.

There are times when a confidence must be revealed because the law requires it. When a person is believed to be a danger to herself or someone else, confidentiality must be broken to protect that person or the person they are threatening to harm. For example, if a person tells you they are going to kill themselves tonight, you are *obligated* to break that confidence and get them the help they need. If they tell you they are going to kill someone else, you are *obligated* to inform those who can protect the intended victim. Most states require the breaking of confidentiality when there is child abuse or even evidence that points to child abuse.

There may come a time when you must break a confidence, but understand that there is a huge "canyonesque" difference in legitimately breaking a confidence and plain, old gossip. The Bible says a lot about gossip. Gossips are to be avoided (1 Tim. 5:13). Gossips break up friendships (Prov. 16:8). The word most often translated "gossip" is a whisperer, a secret-slanderer, or a detractor.

Just because information is true doesn't mean it isn't gossip. When my husband and I were first married, a sweet church lady would come by to visit us regularly. She always brought a dessert with her. She always pumped us for information and tried to give us the latest dirt. We enjoyed the dessert, but not the visit. She would always preface the negative thing she was going to say with these words: "It's not gossip because it is true." It *is* gossip. When you tell something that is not true, that is not gossip—that's lying.

Are you willing to have a part in healing the wounds of people in pain? Can you open your heart and ears to them and then keep your mouth shut in their absence? After the Jordan

River flows into the Dead Sea, the water has no outlet. The water stays there. When people tell you their secrets, become the Dead Sea. Make sure the information stays there.

As the wife of a minister, you are often privileged to such confidences, and people will go to you for information. When our children were in elementary school, a family from church moved in next door. Every time someone came to the house, our neighbor would invite the children over for cookies. After a couple of times, I questioned them about their conversations with her. It was then I realized she was only seeking information. She was not the kindly neighbor I thought her to be. Fortunately, our children never had any "news" for her. We had taught our children from a very early age that whatever was discussed in the house was for family only; we never talked about family to anyone. We also made it a point to see that our children did not hear the confidences shared in our home. We would not burden them with that responsibility.

When it comes to keeping confidences, be sure not to let your pride or ego get in the way. Otherwise, you will find yourself releasing tiny bits of "juicy" information to a select few that you want to impress. If our hearts are not right, then knowing secrets can give us a sense of empowerment and importance. This is wrong. What this information should give us is an awesome sense of responsibility and humility.

There are some people with whom I will never share a confidence. They are nice people and well-intentioned, but whatever goes into their mind comes out of their mouth. I find this sad, not only for myself, but also for them. They are like children who never matured enough to understand the depths of a human heart. As a result, they will never know the mature joy of absolute human trust. Recognizing and accepting responsibility, even for the things we have heard, is the foundation of maturity.

The Scriptures say, "A fool gives full vent to his spirit, but a wise man quietly holds it back" (Prov. 29:11). In World War II, the Navy had a saying, "Loose lips sink ships." What is true in the Navy is true in life. Loose lips sink relationships.

Are there dark corners in your life? Perhaps those dark places are filled with fear or guilt, depression or disappointment, hate or hurt, or anything that pulls down your spirit. Would you want all of those things exposed for the whole world to see? If not, remember this when people share their innermost secrets and feelings with you: "So whatever you wish that others would do to you, do also to them, for this is the Law and the Prophets" (Matt. 7:12). Here are a few more examples from Scripture to think about:

- "Set a guard, O LORD, over my mouth; keep watch over the door of my lips!" (Psa. 141:3).

- "Trusting in a treacherous man in time of trouble is like a bad tooth or a foot that slips" (Prov. 25:19).

- "Whoever guards his mouth preserves his life; he who opens wide his lips comes to ruin" (Prov. 13:3)

- "The wise lay up knowledge, but the mouth of a fool brings ruin near" (Prov. 10:14).

- "When words are many, transgression is not lacking, but whoever restrains his lips is prudent" (Prov. 10:19).

- "A man without self-control is like a city broken into and left without walls" (Prov. 25:28).

- "I tell you, on the day of judgment people will give account for every careless word they speak, for by your words you will be justified, and by your words you will be condemned" (Matt. 12:36-37).

- "Whoever keeps his mouth and his tongue keeps himself out of trouble" (Prov. 21:23).

- "A fool's lips walk into a fight, and his mouth invites a beating. A fool's mouth is his ruin, and his lips are a snare to his soul" (Prov. 18:6-7).

Let's return for a moment to my daughter, Rachel. When trusting a confidence to someone, be sure it is a person you can trust—someone who will keep it in their heart and prayers. I should have known Rachel would probably run and tell her daddy—she was not even three years old yet! She didn't fully understand the importance of keeping a secret or confidence.

Be sure you know the individual in whom you want to confide. Know if she is mature enough to accept the responsibility and trust you place in her. Pray about it before you decide to put your trust in anyone. While I am mentioning it, be sure you are that same trustworthy type of person for someone else.

Have you intentionally or unintentionally betrayed the trust of someone who confided in you? Ask God's forgiveness and take the painful and difficult steps, whatever they may be, to show that you are now committed to a path that is trustworthy. Keep praying; it won't be easy. Remember above all that God can be trusted to keep your confidences, "I know whom I have believed, and I am convinced that he is able to guard until that Day what has been entrusted to me" (2 Tim. 1:12b).

I want to be a person that others can trust. I want to be a person that I can trust. But most of all, I want to be a person God can trust.

6

YOUR RELATIONSHIP WITH ELDERS
Kathy Haynes

*E*ight months pregnant and miserable. Two kind, but unsuspecting souls were watching my four-year-old daughter and two-year-old son. Both children had sweet faces that could fool the most seasoned of mothers. I, however, sat in a room full of men who were deciding if my husband was the right fit for the congregation, of which they were overseers. Initially, I thought it odd that I was invited to sit in on the interview. I had never been asked to do so before. In actuality, I was expected to attend the meeting. After all, they were the ones who had generously made arrangements for my two darling children to be cared for during the process.

Once I stopped worrying about what my tag-team duo was doing to those who had volunteered to watch them (a wonderful elder's wife and her daughter), I began to realize the elders weren't interested only in Tommy and his pulpit abilities. I came to understand they were genuinely interested in how Tommy and I worked together in ministry, as well as how we viewed our roles in marriage and parenting. These leaders wanted to know what I, not Tommy, expected from myself, from Tommy, from them as the leadership, and from the congregation itself. They wanted to know what my vision for the church was and how I could work with them to make the vision a reality.

This group of men expressed what they hoped they could do to help me grow spiritually, not because I was the preacher's wife, but because I would be a member of their flock, their family. Their expectations were nothing more than what they expected from themselves or the rest of the congregation.

As much as I loved the congregations we had served in the past, none of the elderships had ever interviewed me during the hiring process. It was obvious to me this group of men understood the importance of relationships. My apprehension of leaving behind my beloved, small, country town in my native Texas for a city in "Sooner Nation" slipped away. When asked where we saw ourselves in ten years, neither of us hesitated in our answer: "Right here!" Some ministers prefer to stay in a particular place for only a few years, accomplishing smaller, more readily-attainable goals. We explained, however, that this was not our desire.

We wanted stability. We wanted our family to grow spiritually as we ministered to the greater church family. Our intention was to raise our children in this congregation. Our hope was that our children would know the love and support of the same group of Christians throughout their journey toward adulthood. We wanted to see them learn and obey the gospel here. Our desire was for them to become servants, to discover their talents, and to take ownership of their faith under the leadership of this congregation.

Bottom line? We intended to stay for a long time. It was our hope these elders also wanted a lasting relationship.

That was 28 years ago. Two of the men who sat around

the conference table on that fateful day still remain as strong, faithful, exemplary leaders. Others who were in the leadership when we first arrived have since claimed their heavenly reward, moved away, or resigned for health reasons. Other spiritual, godly men have been added and charged with the responsibility of guiding and guarding the family of Christians who meet in Moore. However, the personality of the collective eldership has changed very little. They still desire a relationship with me, the preacher's wife. Just as importantly, I still want that relationship with them.

God has put within us the need for relationships. After all, he placed us in a church family. As preachers' wives, it is natural to develop relationships with other women in the congregation. However, it is equally important to develop and maintain more than a working relationship with our elders. Untapped blessings await us if we choose to enjoy a personal connection with these men who are the overseers of our souls.

WHY IS A RELATIONSHIP WITH YOUR ELDERS IMPORTANT?

Some wives, especially early on in their ministry, may feel intimidated by the thought of spending time with the elders. Some want to fly under the radar and have any communication with the eldership filtered through their husband. Notice the title of this chapter: "Your Relationship with Elders." It does not read "Your Husband's Relationship..." It is important that we develop a relationship with each individual elder, as well as the collective eldership for a number of reasons.

First, it is easy to view elders as employers rather than brothers in Christ. This type of relationship, however, has inherent problems. An us vs. them mentality can develop quickly. When we do not know the men who are leading us, we can often fall prey to suspicion, to taking criticism as a personal attack, questioning every decision, becoming defensive if our husbands are reprimanded, or causing general unrest within the congregation. If we have taken the time to get to know these men on a personal level, we will not view them as bosses, but as brethren. This understanding will enhance not only the working relationship we have, but will cause us to be more aware and thoughtful of the enormous responsibility our eldership has.

In regard to the men who lead us, I often think of Paul's comment in 2 Cor. 11:28. Paul had listed physical trials he had endured, but these external concerns were the least of his worries. Paul says, "There is the daily pressure on me of my anxiety for all the churches." I am among the many for whom the elders are concerned. I am on their prayer list and in their hearts. When we develop a personal relationship with our elders, they become more than employers. They become our guides, confidants, and friends.

Second, unless I allow the elders to know me personally, they cannot address my personal, spiritual needs. Sometimes it is the case that the church is flourishing, but I am floundering. Naturally, I hide it well. I smile, teach my classes, attend every function of the church, study my Bible, pray and yet, I am empty and struggling. If my relationship with my elders is cursory, then I may not feel comfortable going to them in my time of need. I owe it to myself and to the elders to develop a relationship that gives me the confidence I need to go to them with questions and concerns. A relationship of this nature also gives me the opportunity to ask for honest evaluations. What can I do better? How should I have handled a certain situation?

My relationship with the elders is a two-way street. If I maintain and nurture a personal relationship with the elders,

I can also see when they are hurting, have concerns, or need encouragement. Moreover, if I have a concern about a decision they have made, my relationship affords me the liberty of going to them privately, without them feeling challenged and, thus, avoid them becoming defensive. When my elders know my heart, then the avenue for us to help each other is open. If I have sought a relationship based on respect and genuine love, then I will be able to seek solace in the wisdom of godly men during trying times; on the other hand, if I should come to them with a criticism, they will know I am coming to them in love.

Developing a meaningful relationship with my elders helps me understand them and the way they approach their ministry. Knowing them on a personal level will also build my respect for them and the work they have been called to do; this makes them more approachable and helps me become more forgiving when I realize that, before they were elders, they were "human." They were (and still are) just like me. Furthermore, it enables me to view them as wise, but still fallible; without unrealistic expectations, I am less likely to be disappointed if mistakes are made. A personal relationship gives me the good sense to encourage and not condemn them or talk about them in an ungodly way if a situation is mishandled. In matters of doctrine, a close relationship gives me the courage to confront them if necessary. This type of relationship allows for give and take. It brings consistency and confidence to my personal ministry, helps them deal fairly and lovingly with me, and I with them. It also sets a positive tone which leads to peace within the congregation as a whole.

Finally, my relationship with the elders brings balance to my husband's ministry. There may be times when my husband's capacity for compassion is running low, and his patience is spent. He may feel as though no one is listening, as if the elders discount his experience and do not take into consideration ideas or suggestions he may make. It is then that my relationship with the elders can bring my husband back to center. This is actually true of any member's complaint against an elder. When I know my leaders, I can comfort and calm my husband (or member) by reminding him of the hearts of the men with whom he serves. I can defend my elders with confidence, but only if I know them personally.

It is important to develop and maintain relationships with the men who are elders in your congregation. Keep the lines of communication open, develop mutual respect and appreciation, and help each other focus on the needs of the church as a whole. These are all necessary to have a successful, peaceful ministry and, therefore, a vibrant, growing, and sound congregation.

DEVELOPING GOOD RELATIONSHIPS WITH THE ELDERS

The next question, of course, is how do I create such a relationship? While preparing this chapter, I sat down with one of our elders. As we spoke and reminisced about the day his wife and daughter watched my kids during our interview, he mentioned several factors he felt had led to the relationship we currently enjoyed. Among the things he recalled, one in particular stood out the most. The relationship we have has been cultivated over the last 28 years. It did not happen magically just because I was the preacher's wife and he, the elder. It was something we both wanted and worked toward. For the relationship to remain healthy and continue to grow, we both had to put forth the effort. He then went on to share the basic, essential principles he felt had laid the foundation and enhanced our relationship over the years.

Hospitality tops the list. With three children, I was not a candidate for the Good Housekeeping Award. However, our home was always filled with people. One cannot get to know people by shaking their hand and talking for a couple of minutes at services. The close friendships I have didn't happen by sitting next to them in the pew. If you want to know your elders, open your home to them and their families.

Do something together that is not church-related. One of my fondest memories is of a trip we took with an elder and his wife. We learned more about each other in those few days than we ever would have in a church setting. We learned elders have a sense of humor. Laugh with your leaders because, let's face it, some things in ministry you just have to laugh about with someone who understands.

Get to know your elders' wives. So much of what an elder learns about you will come from his wife. Isn't this also true of how we begin to understand the elders themselves? We come to know them more intimately through conversations with their wives. Maybe you don't share the same hobbies or interests. Perhaps you're not a great conversationalist (whereas I could talk all day about sports, but not "girly" topics!). However, you both love men who have accepted stressful ministries. Begin with that common thread. I encourage you to stretch yourself, get out of your comfort zone, and learn new things. Find ways to spend time with your elders' wives and enjoy their wisdom. They have raised children, dealt with frustrated husbands, and lived through it all. These women will laugh and cry with you. They help you see their husbands as men who are not perfect, but are doing their best. As preachers' wives, we do ourselves a disservice if we do not make the time to develop a relationship with the elders' wives.

Honor the elders with your support. If there is a point of contention, handle it in a Christian way by going to them privately. Spreading rumors and gossip is sinful and, ultimately, purposeless. If you are discontent, go to the eldership and get the issue resolved in a loving and prayerful way; speak with respect and kindness. If you make a wonderful suggestion that the elders don't act upon, don't take it personally. If the elders decide to enact a program you expressed misgivings about, don't sabotage the program by talking badly about it; support it. Just as a husband and wife must present a united front when raising children, it is important that the leadership (and yes, you are an unofficial leader among the women) be united, too.

Let's not fool ourselves. The eldership hashes out many disagreements behind closed doors. When these men emerge, however, they have come to an agreement and will proceed in the way they believe, after much prayer and discussion, will be most spiritually beneficial to the congregation as a whole. We should honor them with our support. If an idea fails, they know it. They don't need us telling the congregation, "I told them so!"

Pray, pray, pray. Daily, sincere prayers for these men are needed. In their care are the souls of men, women, and children. Some members in the congregation are struggling with physical, financial, and emotional burdens. There are those who are veering off the path in their spiritual walk. Others are facing divorce or dealing with the death of a loved one. These men are aware of almost every situation, and they need our prayers. Tell them you are praying for them and then—and this is the most important part—do it. Pray for their health, wisdom, and courage.

They also need notes of encouragement; personal, handwritten notes that they can read over and over; tokens of our appreciation they can place on a desk; expressions of our love and concern that can build them up when they are low. Let us not forget that these men, while dealing with the concerns of the congregation, are still trying to lead their own families to heaven. They have personal tragedies and issues they must deal with amidst those of others. There will be times when an elder may not be as responsive as we'd like. During those times, take a step back and consider what may be going on in his life. Encourage your leaders because they also need and deserve comfort and strength in life's trials, just like the rest of us. The title of "elder" does not make them superhuman; it makes them responsible for the continued faithfulness of the congregation they serve in a world of lost souls.

Be involved. By becoming involved in the community and congregation's activities, the eldership will get to know you better and learn what is important to you in your ministry. If you have been asked to be in charge of a certain area or class, keep the elders informed. Ask for ideas, guidance, and approval before proceeding. Be creative in your ministry, looking for ways to serve. Even if you have a young family, make sure you are involved in the church. Although teaching and raising your family is "church work," don't let it be the only thing you do. If you want your relationship with your elders to be a lasting one of mutual trust and respect, let them see you as an individual Christian, not just as an extension of your husband.

As I said at the beginning of this chapter, this is about your relationship with the elders, not your husband's. Just as we will not enter heaven on the coat tails of our husband's good work, we cannot build a relationship with our elders based on what our husband does. If you desire a purposeful relationship with your elders, then you must pursue it. It won't happen simply because your husband is the minister.

BLESSINGS YOU MAY RECEIVE

Being a preacher's wife has its own unique challenges. No two of us will approach this extraordinary life the same way. But each of us can enjoy unparalleled blessings because of the path we have chosen. Developing a successful relationship with our elders can clarify these blessings and cause us to appreciate them even more.

Peace. When the elders, ministers, and unofficial leaders have a good relationship, then peace prevails. That doesn't mean there are no disagreements, but rather that we act like Christians and seek to be peacemakers in tense situations. An understanding relationship with your elders will provide peace for you and your family.

Personal spiritual growth. A personal relationship with the elders helps them know what you need in the quest for your own growth. It gives them insight. Maybe you need a retreat or, perhaps, some time with your husband. It also allows them to help you define and develop your talents. I have been thankful for the eldership and their patience with me, giving me the space and encouragement to develop and grow personally, so that I might be more effective in using the talents I have been given.

Longevity. When I was growing up, I remember telling my mother I didn't want to marry anyone in the military because I didn't like moving. I liked the stability and comfort level that comes with living in one place and getting to really know people. So what did I go and do when I grew up? I married a preacher!

The mindset of ministers and elderships has changed over the years. If a relationship of mutual respect and trust is achieved, not only with the minister but also his wife, then longevity in ministry is a marvelous blessing. I am convinced and confident it is this stability, this consistency and longevity, that contributed to the faithfulness of my three children. All of my children and their spouses are active Christians and still worshipping in the congregation we came to 28 years ago. In fact, our youngest is the youth minister, working alongside his dad. The congregation here, as well as the eldership, had a vested interest in our family. If we have accomplished any good while ministering here, it is largely due to the foresight and patience of an eldership, as well as a congregation, which saw promise in a young minister and his wife and children.

Respect, the ability to accept correction when knowing it comes from a genuine, loving leader, and constant encouragement are among other blessings we could list. May we search for, recognize, and enjoy these blessings to the utmost.

In closing, I would like to assure you that I am not naïve. I am fully aware that not all elderships are as good, sound, peaceful, or qualified as they should be. Nonetheless, on occasion these are the leaders with whom we work, even if the working relationship is not as healthy as it needs to be. If this is the relationship you find yourself in, there are still blessings to be had if you will approach these men with respect, trying to view things from their perspective. You can still grow personally. Patience can be cultivated. Resolve and courage may develop. You can still be a servant, do good works, and encourage others. However, should a situation become unbearable and unworkable for your husband, it is imperative that you still show respect when you part ways. If the departure is a result of doctrinal error, then we must lovingly speak with these men and encourage those who are sound to stand firm. Hopefully, you will never have to endure a trial of this nature, though it is likely some of you will. In this circumstance, it is even more important to develop a personal relationship with your elders because it is the only way you could possibly have a positive impact on them and, perhaps, cause them to turn back to the biblical truths God has given us.

In 1 Cor. 13, Paul urged Christians to learn what love would and would not do. The charge laid at the feet of these men—known as elders, overseers, and shepherds—is one that we cannot fully understand as women. This role is one God reserved only for mature, godly, wise, and spiritual men; it is a cross borne by courageous men with tender and compassionate hearts. Much like Moses, they endure grumblings, false accusations, and misperceptions. Yet, they lead because of their love for God and his family.

As preachers' wives, let us ease their burden by supporting them with the unfailing love of which Paul wrote. May we be faithful and constant in our pursuit to develop a relationship with these men so that it will strengthen our ministry here and unite us eternally in heaven.

7

HAVING FUN WITH HOSPITALITY
Judi Dean

A young mother anxiously put the finishing touches on the table that would seat twelve guests. She had been cooking and cleaning all day, trying to make everything perfect. When all the guests arrived and were seated, she asked her young son to say the blessing. He replied, "But Mom, I don't know what to say." "Just say what you have heard us say," she told him. So her sweet son began his blessing, "Lord, why did I invite all these people over!?" You may have heard this widely-circulated story, or better yet....you may have lived it! The lady of the house was most likely the preacher's wife, right?

When we enter into the world of a preacher's wife, sometimes we feel as if we are expected to have people in our home all the time, like it's some sort of job requirement. I like to look at it in a different light. As the minister's wife, I have a greater opportunity to open my home to others. I might be able to invite someone over, especially members, and allow them to see that we are just people, too! It can dissolve preconceived ideas formed by some members.

We often think of hospitality as only referring to hosting a gathering in your home. It can also include taking a meal to someone in need. It could be a newcomer, someone who is sick, or those experiencing the loss of a loved one. I like to keep some things made and in the freezer for those times when someone needs a meal right away. Soup is easy to make and freeze. Casseroles and pies can be made and frozen ahead of time. Taking food to others in their own home is a great way to break the ice with some people. If they are a little shy about getting together, you can still let them know you care.

Hospitality can also be opening your home as a place of rest for those from out of town, such as a youth group or visiting preacher. In 2 Kings 4, we read of the Shunnamite woman and her husband who built a room just for Elisha, knowing he would come through their town regularly. Having people stay in your home gives you the opportunity to get to know one another on a more personal level. Having been on the receiving end of this several times, it is a very welcoming gesture and helps build strong friendships.

But since hospitality is generally thought of as hosting others for a meal or fellowship, we will devote the majority of our remaining text to this topic.

Why do we get so worried and anxious about hosting others in our home? Maybe we feel inadequate as a cook or housekeeper. Maybe it is because we have been invited places that set a standard we do not feel we can live up to. Do we feel we won't be "good enough"? When I hear these excuses, I can't help but think that we are putting way too much pressure on ourselves and underestimating the integrity of our guests.

I guess I have always enjoyed having people over to our house. It is something I grew up with, and it has provided me with many fond memories of our friends spending Sunday afternoons with us at our house or theirs. Every time there was a visiting preacher at our congregation, my mom would cook a big meal and invite his family over. Other times, it was just a big group coming over for a "chicken bog" or fish fry. What I remember most about these occasions was how much fun we had. I don't remember being told that we had to act a certain way or that the house had to be perfect. I don't remember it being a "big deal." It was just something we did. It was normal.

Normal, however, changes from year to year. What was normal for us has been lost in the shuffle. What is the shuffle? Jobs, practices, games, appointments—you name it, we shuffle them all. But I think we can learn to find hospitality in the shuffle again, to have lots of fun, and to fulfill God's will at the same time. Let's look at what hospitality is, how it fits into God's plan, and how it can be a blessing both to our lives and those around us.

Hospitality is defined as "the act or practice of one who is hospitable; the reception of strangers or guests without reward, or with kind and generous liberality." The definition itself implies true acts of Christianity. As Christians, we are meant to love others: "A new commandment I give to you, that you love one another: just as I have loved you, you also are to love one another" (John 13:34). We all know this is not just an emotional love, but an active love that treats others well without expecting anything in return.

We are not only commanded to love, but also to be hospitable. What a great opportunity hospitality gives us to show active love. Romans 12:13 teaches, "Share with the Lord's people who are in need. Practice hospitality" (NIV). This is not a suggestion. The writer was divinely inspired to tell the Roman Christians what they were supposed to do. Not only do we have a direct command, we also have biblical examples of hospitality. Let's look at a few of them and see what we can learn from each situation.

First, in Gen. 18:1-8, Abraham and Sarah received three guests who came unannounced to their home. We see in this story that, after Abraham invited them to stay for something to eat, he then went and told Sarah to prepare something for them. Can you imagine how you would feel if your husband sprang that on you? But she did not complain. She began preparing what they had to offer and eventually the men were served. Now that's hospitality! The outcome of this story is the beginning of the ultimate promise that we benefit from today. The men had come with great news. Abraham and Sarah were blessed with a son whose seed ultimately was our Lord and Savior! What might have happened if Abraham had not invited them to stay? Or what might have happened if Sarah had refused to cook for them?

In my judgment, the greatest lesson from this passage is that hospitality can be a "spur of the moment" event. It does not always have to mean a lot of preparation. Abraham and Sarah filled a need. They did not know that these men had come specifically to see them and to bless them. Abraham even said, "Let me get you something to eat so that you can be refreshed and then be on your way." He just thought they were passing through, yet he and Sarah showed hospitality. We may need to show "spur of the moment" hospitality when we have the chance. Who knows whether that opportunity will ever be afforded again?

Another great example of hospitality is found in Gen. 43:16-34 with the story of Joseph and his brothers. We all know how his brothers had treated him when he was just a youth. But when it was Joseph's turn to retaliate, he chose not to. He prepared a feast for his brothers and later in the story revealed to them that he was their brother, Joseph. He even told them in Gen. 50:20, "As for you, you meant evil against me, but God meant it for good."

What is the lesson here? There will be occasions when

people will be in your home with whom you don't have the closest relationship. Maybe even someone at church who has made a comment that hurt your feelings or someone whose personality rubs you the wrong way. Be a Joseph. Be hospitable, even in the face of difficulty. Who knows? Your relationship might change considerably once you have them in your home and show them that you care. Think long and hard like the little boy in the prayer. "Why did I invite all these people over?" What is your motive? Are you having them over to show off your house? Do you want them to see what a good cook you are? Are you trying to make a good impression as the minister's wife? If any of these are true, your motives are wrong. Remember the definition we gave for hospitality? The reception of strangers or guests *without reward*! It's not, "What's in it for me?" It's, "How can I best serve?" "What needs can I fill?" "How can we get to know one another better so that we can better serve one another?"

You know I can't leave out Mary and Martha! It is probably the story that comes to mind the most when we think about hospitality. Luke 10:38-42 shows how to be hospitable to the Most Honored Guest. It is a short story, and we often look at Martha in a very harsh way. If you look at the very beginning of this story, Martha is the one who invited Jesus into her home. She was "distracted with much serving" or "distracted with the everyday chores of serving." But this doesn't make her a bad person. When she asked Jesus to tell Mary to help, he let her know the reason he was there. If you think about it, we would probably be like Martha if we knew Jesus were coming to our home. We would want everything to be perfect!

Hopefully, in the remainder of this chapter, we can address some practical solutions to our hesitancy when it comes to hospitality. There are three key points that I want us to consider.

KEEP IT SIMPLE

The first is *simplicity*! It does not always have to be a big ordeal. Our hospitality is not in competition with that of anyone else. We are not doing it for show. We are doing it as a service to others, so keep it simple! Simple suggestions:

- Soup/sandwich night
- Taco night
- Fast food (everyone grab their own and come over)
- Desserts only
- Salad bar (each brings an ingredient)
- Build your own sub sandwich (everyone bring a topping)

It is really simple to plan an evening at your home and just have everyone bring a dish. You will find that most people will ask you what they can bring anyway. Have some ideas in mind. If it is soup/sandwich night, you make the soup and have everyone bring sandwiches and dessert. For taco night, have everyone bring a different topping. It does not have to be difficult. These kinds of events make it easy for families with children because the guests can bring something they know their children will eat!

These are also easy events to plan spur of the moment. Invite some folks on Sunday morning to come over after the evening service. They have the afternoon to prepare what they are going to bring. And you don't have time to back out! Use paper plates and plastic cups!

Just remember to keep it simple. This will make you feel more comfortable as a hostess, and your guests will feel comfortable knowing it is something simple and casual. Anything that makes it a little easier for you will also help your guests feel that they aren't a burden! When you invite company over, put the emphasis on "getting together" instead of what you are eating.

MIX IT UP

The second key to good hosting is *variety*. Don't have the same kind of gathering every time you have folks over. Mix it up a little. Here are a few suggestions:

- Rook tournament
- Game night
- Birthday bash
- Holiday theme parties
- Ladies brunch
- Cook-out
- Potluck
- Elegant dinner

When planning gatherings, try to vary the age of your guests. We try to have the 39ers over once a year for a potluck dinner and entertainment. These are the folks over 55 who we have bring a dish before we all eat together and enjoy musical entertainment from some of our members.

At other times, we have hosted the college group for a Christmas party. They all brought finger foods and gifts to play Dirty Santa! What a great way to get to know each other! Especially when someone takes away that gift you really wanted! Better yet, they can't believe the preacher would actually take a gift away! They learn a side of your family that they need to know: approachable, human, loving, and with a sense of humor!

When we hosted a rook tournament, we had all ages mixed together. We had serious rook players and some who came to learn. We even gave out certificates to the winners, the whiners, and the cheaters (just for fun!).

For several years, when we were at a smaller congregation, we had what we called a "birthday bash." I got this idea from my sister, Cynthia Guy, who is also a minister's wife. On the fourth Sunday of each month, we invited everyone in the congregation that had a birthday that month to come over to our house. We provided the birthday cake and everyone else brought finger food. We almost always played "Encore," which is a game that can be played with lots of people on a team! It was about music, so it would cover several genres with oldies, as well as new stuff. Everyone knows a song or two of some kind. All ages had a ball!

I think this is a good place to make another observation. As our kids were growing up, they always had a part in these events. We never told them that we had to do this or that they had to behave a certain way because we were the preacher's family and had to set an example. They could see this was something we wanted to do out of love for God's people. They always understood that what we did was because we were, and are, Christians.

Now, although I do feel it is important to keep it simple, now and then it is fun to have a smaller dinner party or a more complicated, elegant dinner. One of our young ladies was leaving for two years for the Dominican Republic to do missionary work. Before she left, we invited her and her grandparents over for a sit-down, elegant dinner, complete with personalized place cards. It was just a way to show our appreciation to her and give her a big full meal before she entered a different culture of food.

Stan and I will sometimes invite a new couple or two along with someone who has been a member for many years. This gives both of them a chance to get to know one another in a small group setting. We try to talk about what they do for a living. We ask about their extended family and tell about our own. You can learn a lot about someone just conversing over dinner.

So you see, a variety can make your gatherings more interesting and give you the chance to be with more people in the congregation, young and old. So try something new!

START NOW

The last key point I want to cover is that you do not need to keep putting it off. We keep saying we are going to have some people over, or that we meant to invite them and just didn't get around to it. I have often urged women in ladies' day lessons to go ahead and invite someone and then plan everything else; this way, you do what seems to be the hardest part first. Once you invite someone, you *have* to follow through. And don't be discouraged if they cannot come when you invite them. Invite someone else for this time and come back to these folks later. Don't give up! Somebody will be able to come.

We always seem to have time for everything else in our lives. We plan for piano lessons, kids' sports, classes—even favorite TV shows. We plan for shopping, eating out, movies, and birthdays. We need to plan for some of God's things. We are his body here on earth. We are his hands and feet. He always has time for those in need. Shouldn't we as well? Let me challenge you to look at your calendar right now and start planning. It will be a blessing to you and to those you invite. Most of all, it will bring glory to God.

How important is hospitality? Let's look at a few passages from God's Word that will give us some insight. In 1 Tim. 5:10, the widows that qualified as "widows indeed" were required to be hospitable. In Tit. 1:8, a requirement for elders is that they must be hospitable. First Peter 4:9 tells Christians to "show hospitality to one another without grumbling." Hebrews 13:1-2 says, "Let brotherly love continue. Do not neglect to show hospitality to strangers, for thereby some have entertained angels unawares."

These are not the only passages we have that impress upon us the importance of hospitality. Look at the example Jesus left for us in Matt. 14:14-21. Here we see Jesus' compassion for those who came to hear him. He fed them—all five thousand of them. I'm sure you've never had to feed that many at one time! In John 21, after Jesus had risen from the dead, he cooked fish and bread for the disciples to eat. They had been out fishing all night and were tired. These were some of Jesus' closest friends, so he attended to their needs. Over and over, he helped the sick, the lame, the hungry, and sinners. As Christ's body, these are the same people we need to help.

How important is hospitality? One more passage will show us that it is of the utmost importance.

> When the Son of Man comes in his glory, and all the angels with him, then he will sit on his glorious throne. Before him will be gathered all the nations, and he will separate people one from another as a shepherd separates the sheep from the goats. And he will place the sheep on his right, but the goats on the left. Then the King will say to those on his right, "Come, you who are blessed by my Father, inherit the kingdom prepared for you from the foundation of the world. For I was hungry and you gave me food, I was thirsty and you gave me drink, I was a stranger and you welcomed me, I was naked and you clothed me, I was sick and you visited me, I was in prison and you came to me." Then the righteous will answer him, saying,

"Lord, when did we see you hungry and feed you, or thirsty and give you drink? And when did we see you a stranger and welcome you, or naked and clothe you? And when did we see you sick or in prison and visit you?" And the King will answer them, "Truly, I say to you, as you did it to one of the least of these my brothers, you did it to me."

Then he will say to those on his left, "Depart from me, you cursed, into the eternal fire prepared for the devil and his angels. For I was hungry and you gave me no food, I was thirsty and you gave me no drink, I was a stranger and you did not welcome me, naked and you did not clothe me, sick and in prison and you did not visit me." Then they also will answer, saying, "Lord, when did we see you hungry or thirsty or a stranger or naked or sick or in prison, and did not minister to you?" Then he will answer them, saying, "Truly, I say to you, as you did not do it to one of the least of these, you did not do it to me." And these will go away into eternal punishment, but the righteous into eternal life.

— Matt. 25:31-46

Christ says hospitality is important, and this is true for every Christian. Therefore, it is important for the minister's wife. We need to take every opportunity we have to "show kindness to strangers and guests without expecting a reward." It will greatly enhance the work your husband does as the minister. It will help you grow as a Christian. Moreover, it is so much fun! And the lesson we just learned in Matt. 25 teaches that we will receive a reward—eternal life!

8

DEALING WITH LONELINESS
Carrie Voss

Have you ever thought about what makes us lonely and discouraged at times? When talking to fellow preachers' wives about this subject, there are a few reasons that were quite common. The first reason that loneliness and discouragement creep into our lives is because of unrealistic expectations that are placed on us by fellow Christians in our congregation. The second reason is when we endure difficult times in life, but they seem to be magnified if you're married to the preacher. Are we really that different from other Christians and what they go through? How can we safeguard our heart and attitude so we don't feel lonely and discouraged?

UNREALISTIC EXPECTATIONS FROM OTHERS

The first common reason for preachers' wives feeling lonely and discouraged is because of unrealistic expectations put on us by fellow Christians in regards to being a preacher's wife, mother, and overall Christian. If you've been a preacher's wife for a few years, you've surely heard "our former preacher's wife was so good at (fill in the blank)." While they may not mean to hurt your feelings intentionally, you feel that pressure to live up to the talents of all the previous preachers' wives at your congregation. Another example that you may have encountered is criticism of your personality. Some members may have the opinion that you should be more outgoing or friendly, while others may think you are too enthusiastic. These comments can be conflicting, and you might start to question who you really are and how you should act. You may have experienced such opinions on various topics in your life such as:

- You should not work outside the home.
- Your hairstyle is too short, too long, or too outdated.
- Your clothes are too old-fashioned or too expensive.
- You wear too much make-up or not enough.
- You're too skinny or too overweight.
- Your children should attend public school, not a private school or be homeschooled, so they can be a light to the world.
- You discipline your children too harshly or not enough.
- You don't teach enough Bible classes, or you teach too many classes and don't give others an opportunity to teach.
- You don't cook enough food for fellowship meals, or your meals aren't that tasty.
- You don't visit, call, or send enough cards to the elderly and sick.
- Your home isn't as clean as it should be.

- Your home is too big and expensive.
- Your furniture is too expensive and nice.
- You go on too many vacations.
- Your car is too old or messy, or you shouldn't have a new, expensive car.
- You should have more children, or you have too many children.
- You should walk down the aisle with your husband after the sermon.
- You shouldn't have close friends in the congregation because you don't want to appear partial to others.

If we listened to and took to heart every opinion every member had of what they thought a preacher's wife should do or not do, we'd exhaust ourselves from trying to please everyone. Because we are no different than any other Christian woman, we are guaranteed to fail in meeting their expectations. We could spend much of our time trying to correct the misconception of those man-made roles, but a more productive solution would be to know what the Bible says about living a Christian life and following those expectations. If we are confident in our beliefs, then we are less likely to let doubt creep in and make us believe we aren't fulfilling the "preacher's wife role." Satan is looking for ways to make us question our ability as a preacher's wife. I know I would've saved a great deal of worry and insecurity in my earlier days as a preacher's wife if I understood that there are no biblical requirements for a preacher's wife, no matter how critical others are of our role.

GOD'S EXPECTATIONS OF US

Our requirements are the same of any Christian woman, and everything else is just an opinion. It's important to be humble and do a self-evaluation of ourselves when others approach us with criticism to see if we truly need to work on something. However, the expectations we need to meet are the ones God has defined in Scripture alone. Whenever you're questioning yourself, your role, and whether you're being a "good enough" preacher's wife, look at the attributes below concerning God's expectation of you and spend your time and energy working on these traits, rather than what others think you should be:

- Keeper of the house
- Faithful wife
- Control the tongue
- Kind
- Demonstrate love
- Forgiving
- Patient
- Joyful
- Demonstrate pure thinking
- Faithful
- Self-control
- Gentle
- Obedient
- Courageous
- Encourager
- Honest
- Grateful

- Wise
- Pray
- Study the Bible
- Humble
- Hard working
- Peaceful
- Sincere
- Trustworthy
- Demonstrate goodness
- Content
- Generous
- Wise
- Show compassion

ENDURING DIFFICULT TIMES IN LIFE

The second most common reason for preachers' wives feeling lonely and discouraged is because of the circumstances we face in life. What would you do if a member confided in you that she was really discouraged in her spiritual life and just dreaded coming to Bible class and worship? What would you do if a member confided in you that she had gone to a counselor to get help with her marital struggles? What would you do if a couple confided in you that they were questioning God's love because their child was killed in a car accident or was diagnosed with an incurable disease? Would you think of them any different? Most likely, you'll answer those questions with a resounding "No." You'd pray with them, comfort them, and keep it confidential if they requested it, right? After all, Scripture says, "Bear one another's burdens, and so fulfill the law of Christ" (Gal.

6:2). What if the tables were turned and one of those scenarios was about you? Do you think this verse would apply to you, or do you think members subconsciously add "unless you're the preacher's wife" to the end of that verse? Do we set ourselves apart, or do others set us apart, despite our efforts to be one of them? Often, preachers' wives feel like we are the only ones going through these life struggles because everyone's eyes seem to be on our family. We are not immune to trials and tribulations in life. Below are some examples of the challenges all Christians might face during different seasons of life:

Family Problems
- Unfaithful family members
- Adult children unfaithful and left the church
- Death of a parent
- Death of a child
- Death of a grandparent
- Empty nest
- Special needs children
- Caring for aged parents
- Live far away from family and don't get to see them often

Health Problems
- Miscarriage
- Infertility
- Cancer
- Diagnosed with long-term illness

Financial Problems
- Job loss

- Job relocation
- Debt
- Can't afford college education for kids

Friend Problems

- Left out/no friends due to beliefs on particular topics
- Mocked and gossiped about
- Can't trust anyone because they'll tattle to members and elders
- Most people have been friends for years at my congregation, and they won't let me in and include me

All of the above situations happen to faithful Christians as well. It's important to recognize that we are not the only ones who go through trials in life. Most Christians go through these same struggles, and we should not feel ashamed to ask for help and prayers. You may feel like all eyes are on your family, and that may be true to some degree. But that doesn't mean you're not human and don't have feelings just like everyone else. Find others to help bear your burdens. If they are acting as a Christian should, they will pray for you and be there for you, and they will not use your situation against you.

You can use your circumstances to help others as well. If you've been through a miscarriage, the death of a parent, or any of the situations listed above, you know firsthand what someone else is going through. Don't let the opportunity pass you by to be there for them. Use the trials in your life as a ministry to others.

WHAT HURTS THE MOST

I've been a preacher's wife for over fifteen years, and I can tell you from firsthand experience and from talking with many other preachers' wives that the most painful thing we go through is isolation from church members. There are certain situations that only preachers' wives go through and that only fellow preachers' wives can truly understand. When your husband has taken a stand against an unpopular topic, or he has been accused of saying or doing something that is untrue, it leaves your family ostracized, and it can cause indescribable loneliness and pain. How do you handle it when you go to worship, and a member walks right past you, ignoring your kind greeting? What do you do when you are purposely left out of a planning meeting for an upcoming ladies, youth, or congregational activity? How do you handle the unkindness outwardly shown to you by those who make it known that your husband is not the one whom they wanted hired? When your husband comes home discouraged from an elders' meeting or a men's business meeting and is considering leaving the ministry, what do you say to him to encourage him? What do you do when your children have been told by a member that their father is the reason the congregation's attendance is low, and the church would be better off if your family moved somewhere else? What do you do when a family makes the decision to stop attending and blames you and your husband? These are just a few examples of what I've witnessed myself or fellow preachers' wives have experienced. It hurts—*a lot*.

Meditate on God's Word and Pray

If you've ever experienced anything like this at your congregation, the most important thing you should do is go to

God in prayer and study the Scriptures to make sure you are reacting with the proper attitude. The church walls are not immune to Satan, and he's seeking to turn Christian attitudes into hateful attitudes. In some circumstances, he's succeeded. Don't return slander with slander, but pray for them and show them kindness just like Christ did when he was persecuted and falsely accused. In times like these, I especially find it necessary to read and study about people from the Bible who experienced such isolation and criticism. The pages of the Bible are filled with people who did the right thing, even when they faced persecution, false accusations, and trials in their life.

Another way to keep your focus on God during trying times is to keep Bible verses in plain sight and refer to them numerous times a day. Put them on your refrigerator, in your Bible, taped to your bathroom mirror, on a sticky note by your computer, in the dashboard of your car, or anywhere else that will remind you to keep your focus on God. Here are few examples:

- "Count it all joy, my brothers, when you meet trials of various kinds, for you know that the testing of your faith produces steadfastness. And let steadfastness have its full effect, that you may be perfect and complete, lacking in nothing" (Jas. 1:2-4).

- "No temptation has overtaken you that is not common to man. God is faithful, and he will not let you be tempted beyond your ability, but with the temptation he will also provide the way of escape, that you may be able to endure it" (1 Cor. 10:13).

- "Not only that, but we rejoice in our sufferings, knowing that suffering produces endurance, and endurance produces character, and character produces hope" (Rom. 5:3-4).

- "I can do all things through him who strengthens me" (Phil. 4:13).

- "And we know that for those who love God all things work together for good, for those who are called according to his purpose" (Rom. 8:28).

- "Trust in the LORD with all your heart, and do not lean on your own understanding. In all your ways acknowledge him, and he will make straight your paths" (Prov. 3:5-6).

Befriend Fellow Preachers' Wives

I strongly urge you to find fellow preachers' wives to confide in. Many years had passed before I understood the importance of seeking out friendship with other preachers' wives. Don't go to them for the purpose of slandering members in your congregation, but with a sincere heart in hoping they can give insight and advice on how to handle situations in a Christ-like way. They've walked in your shoes, and they will be able to give you rational advice from an outsider's point of view. Make a list of all of the congregations in your area and the name of the minister, then find the preachers' wives on Facebook or contact their husbands for their email addresses. Decide on a lunch or dinner meeting, and you will find yourself blessed by the fellowship, even if only one or two can attend. You will have to put forth some effort in making this happen, but the spiritual benefits will be worth it. You may live in a town with very few or no other congregations nearby. Technology can be your greatest asset in reaching out to fellow preachers' wives. Facebook groups, email, blogs, podcasts, and online audio sermons are at your fingertips if you seek them out.

Attending conferences, retreats, workshops and ladies' days will surely give your discouraged attitude a boost. Also, it will help you meet new people and learn more from God's Word.

A preacher's wife retreat is held each year where preachers' wives from all over the country come together to fellowship. Lifelong friendships have been made at the retreat, as well as conferences such as Polishing the Pulpit. If you seek out events such as these, your outlook on life will be much more optimistic because you're surrounded by those who are like-minded.

Focus on the Positives

You've heard the expression that it takes one thousand praises to erase one criticism. Does that expression seem to fit the description for the praise and criticism you've received as a preacher's wife? It sure applies to me. On days when I'm feeling lonely and discouraged, those critical words from others in my past fifteen years as a preacher's wife come to the forefront of my memory. It's almost as if they happened yesterday, and it can change my attitude in an instant. When you're tempted to focus on the negative, I have a few ideas that might help. First, keep all of the encouraging letters and cards that you receive from others in a box or place in your home that's easily accessible. Write Phil. 4:8 on the outside of the box. Read them when you're discouraged and even when you're not discouraged.

Keep a notebook with a running list of the encouraging words and actions that fellow Christians have demonstrated over the years. A member might drop a container of strawberries by your house, you might be invited to a member's house for dinner, your family may be given a monetary gift from a member right before you leave for vacation, you might be praised by someone about your child's behavior, someone may make a positive comment to you about your husband's sermon—the list goes on and on. If you are consistent with keeping the notebook up-to-date, you'll find yourself quite busy as you focus on the positives instead of the negatives.

Keep in contact with the encouraging members from your former congregations. When your family leaves a congregation, don't cut all ties with them just because you're not in constant contact with them or you don't live near them anymore. They may need your encouragement just as much as you need theirs. It's difficult to keep in touch with everyone, but your effort will have lasting effects in your life and theirs as well.

Let the Past Go

Do you dwell on things you've done or said to others in the past? Do you dwell on what others have done to you or said to you in the past? We are all going to make mistakes as preachers' wives, and we will have others transgress against us. While we can't unspeak an unkind word, we can ask for forgiveness from God and the person we hurt, even if it occurred years ago. We are going to come in contact with numerous people throughout our years as a preacher's wife, and that gives us plenty of opportunities to make mistakes. While we may strive always to have seasoned words, we may sin and use our tongues for evil at various times in our lives. In turn, we may have others who hurt us with their words and actions.

Don't let an opportunity to seek forgiveness from others pass by because of pride. We all sin and are sinned against, but we need to be humble enough to admit our wrongdoing. If someone comes to us asking for forgiveness, we need to forgive them and be sure not to hold it against them in the future. One of the common struggles I personally have and that other preachers' wives have told me is that they often do not have closure once they leave a congregation. Misunderstandings and words spoken because of frustration can damage relationships with fellow Christians. Hurt feelings can still be festering if they have never been dealt with, even if you have moved miles away. I urge you to seek resolution by writing a letter, sending an email, calling them on the phone, or meeting them face to face. We should all hope to see them in heaven one day, and we never want to hinder their faith.

Paul writes in Phil. 3:13-14, "Brothers, I do not consider that I have made it my own. But one thing I do: forgetting what lies behind and straining forward to what lies ahead, I press on toward the goal for the prize of the upward call of God in Christ Jesus." What if Paul dwelt on all of the horrific words and actions he had committed before he was converted? Do you have anyone in your past that you need to make peace with, or do you have anyone in your past that has hurt you and you need to let go of those painful memories?

Stay Strong

At the end of our lives, it won't matter what opinions others have of the life we lived as a preacher's wife. May it be our goal in life to stay focused on God's commandments and standards that he sets for us in the Bible and not by the standards set by people of what they think a preacher's wife should be.

Focus on the positives of being married to the preacher; there are so many! Thank God daily that you are married to someone who has devoted his life to teaching and preaching the gospel. Continually strive to find ways to encourage your husband as he does the most important job in the world.

We are going to be dealt some unfair cards in life, and we may not ever get to explain our side of the story for the sake of unity in the church. But if life were perfect, we wouldn't look forward to heaven (2 Pet. 3:13).

One of my favorite quotes since my teen years has been, "Whatever is right is not always popular. Whatever is popular is not always right." Don't be afraid to stand up for what you know is right, even if you're the only one standing up, and even if that means your family may face persecution.

9

MENTORING THE NEXT GENERATION
Jami Roberts

Have you ever thought to yourself, "Is anyone listening?" You know, that feeling of, "I'm pouring out my soul here, people, and I don't seem to have your attention!"? I know you have, because we all have. A few years ago, I felt a deep conviction that I wasn't doing all I could to teach the younger women (cf. Tit. 2:3-5). I was watching the younger women in our congregation struggle spiritually, as teens, as parents, or in their marriages. They struggled like everyone else in so many day-to-day activities.

I was about forty years old at the time and overflowing with wisdom. I had recently graduated from the Bear Valley Bible Institute; I'd been married around twenty years and had five amazing children. It was time for the younger women to listen to me. It was time for them to allow me to bless their lives. So I started a ladies' Bible class, hoping to make myself feel better. Well, it backfired because the turn out was low and not very many were really committed to attending regularly. I decided maybe I wasn't connected enough to them and started having them in my home to try to build relationships. That really didn't go over the way I wanted it to either. I was building relationships, but I still felt like no one wanted to hear from my deep well of wisdom. All I wanted to do was obey God and be a blessing to those willing to learn from me.

I was baffled by the lack of "obedience" in the women surrounding me. I was astonished that they didn't want to improve their lives and draw closer to the Lord. I mean, obviously they had some deep spiritual issues that needed to be worked on because they weren't willing to listen to the Word of God that came from my mouth. So I started praying about it. "Lord," I would say, "help these women have soft hearts and be willing to listen to me so that I can fulfill your command to teach them. Help them put aside their pride and selfishness to be willing to sit at the feet of an older woman. Help them see the importance of making changes in their lives so they might resemble me, who in turn looks like you."

You get the picture. I was *so* focused on me, my "mission," and what I needed that I was not really looking to help guide other women. I wanted a specific bunch to glean from my teaching. I was narrow-minded and judgmental. I was trying to shove everyone into a box that looked just like mine. It took me about ten years of frustrating myself before I realized that I was actually praying incorrectly; I had been too focused on *me*. I didn't even realize how prideful I had become! I was using the "mantle" of "preacher's wife" in a way that could have actually harmed the church. (And I had always been one to say, "'Preacher's wife' isn't a title; I'm married to a preacher, that's all.) Shame on me! I had to make some changes if I wanted to make a difference in my life, let alone anyone else's. So I did, I still am, and God continues to hit me between the eyes with opportunities. Let me share with you what has worked for me.

1. I CHANGED THE WAY I WAS PRAYING!

I realized that I was praying in a way that seemed to be focused outward and not inward. I should have asked God to make changes in me so that I could see more clearly and be better prepared for the opportunities he would send my way. I started praying for God to send me opportunities (Gal. 6:10) and for my eyes to be open to those opportunities. I prayed that he would give me a better understanding of those opportunities. I needed to understand that every person that came through my life didn't need a sermon, but rather for me to care about them; they needed hope. I prayed that he would use me to strengthen the kingdom (2 Thess. 2:17). I also prayed that he would help me remove any selfish thinking in me so that I could work toward glorifying God (Matt. 5:16).

Boy, did he answer that prayer! I started teaching in the women's program at the Bear Valley Bible Institute. I encouraged a friend to start a daily devotional website for women (comefillyourcup.com) and started an annual woman's retreat to dig deeper into God's Word. I was invited to be a part of Higher Ground, a camp for teen girls. My husband, Wayne, and I started traveling, sharing our marriage seminar, "His Shoes, Her Shoes." Opportunities came pouring in! (Disclaimer: I cannot guarantee the same kinds of opportunities for you because you aren't me. God will use you differently, focusing on your own talents and strengths.)

My prayer life improved drastically! I was finally working on Tami! And when I worked on Tami, God used me for his glory. I learned the importance of turning everything over to him and trusting him to be in charge.

I also started praying that he would mold me to be like Jesus and show me, through his Word, how to be compassionate, to truly care for others, to show that I do hurt when others hurt. Most importantly for me, I prayed that God would help me to see not only the sins of those around me, but to see their hurting lives and needs. He has *totally* changed the way I see others! He has helped me remember to see those in Christ as new creatures. I no longer see just their flaws; I see Jesus as well (2 Cor. 5:16-17). He has helped me remember to see those in the world as lost! They don't know how to behave, and they have no hope because they don't know him (1 John 3:6). When I started looking at others differently, I could finally see their needs more clearly and how I could show them that I cared, which led to multiple opportunities!

2. I HAD TO BE WILLING TO LOOK UP!

Once my prayer-life changed, God showered me with opportunities, but not where I thought they would be. I kept thinking that the younger women, the ones I was meant to teach, were the ones sitting in worship with me. I did not realize that when I looked up and beyond the walls of the building just how many young women, everywhere, were *starving* for someone with which to talk. Working through other congregations, as well as through social media, I was used by God to touch the lives of women everywhere.

Teaching at the school in Bear Valley keeps me in touch with women all over the place. I try to be an encourager for them, just as they are for me. For example, through Come Fill Your Cup, I have met women from all over the U.S. When registration opens up each year for the retreat, I love to see the age range. We have women from all age groups. We had one member this year who thanked the older women for making the sacrifice to come to a retreat and share their wisdom with the younger women. I'm telling you, there are women out there starving for the wisdom of their elders!

Through Higher Ground, I keep in touch with teenagers and those who have graduated high school. This is another age group that is famished for someone to take their hand and show them how to walk in the light. They do not want someone to simply give them a "Scripture lesson," but rather someone who cares enough to take their hand, touch their lives, and help them on the journey. Social media is an amazing way to stay in touch with these women, because it is such a fixture of their new world.

Through "His Shoes, Her Shoes," I have met women all over the U.S. that need someone to talk to about their marriage. They need someone that won't condemn them for what they aren't doing, but will lift them up. They need someone that will make them feel like maybe, just maybe, their marriage is not doomed. Moreover, they need someone that will let them know that they have "been there, done that," and that it is all "normal."

Don't pen yourself in! Look up! God has plans to use you; it just may not be *where* you originally imagined.

3. I HAD TO RELAX AND BE MYSELF!

So many times, preachers' wives have a mental picture of who they are supposed to be, or they let others try to shape them into what they think a preacher's wife should look like. We let that affect how we reach out to others. Even those of us that understand the concept of "we are all Christians" can be sucked into trying to fit the mold. Usually, I am pretty good at being myself with women, or I hope I am. The first time I spoke to the teen girls at Higher Ground, however, I was so scared! I remembered being a teen and having a judgmental attitude towards "old women." When I started speaking, I watched as their facial expressions shifted and, in turn, totally changed up what I was going to say. I had to stop teaching and just talk to them. I started just being Tami and found out that they loved me anyway. I've come to realize that when I'm with teens or children, it's easier to be myself. They love me even more when my crazy side comes out.

After the whole "teen girl" awakening moment, I realized I had also been "preaching" to my generation, as well as my elders. I decided to relax and just talk to people, to let God's Word flow through my heart and from my mouth. I would not succumb to that overwhelming pressure to "fix" everyone, but rather just be there for them. More importantly, I would be there as Tami, with all my goofiness and flaws.

People will know if you are being genuine. Learn to let go and let the real you come out. If you come across as this perfect, rigid, Christian woman, then they are not going to feel a connection with you. Just be you!

4. I HAD TO PUT MY PRIDE ASIDE!

As women started turning to me with their struggles and pain, I realized that for me to be able to comfort them, I needed them to know me in turn. I needed them to know what struggles I have been through or even the ones I'm dealing with now. I need them to know when I truly have "been there, done that" (2 Cor. 1:3-4).

So often, we hide our troubles. We want to appear as super Christians. I believe that our pride is what keeps us from lowering our shield. After all, we don't want anyone to think less of us. Now, don't get me wrong; I don't keep a list of my sins taped to my forehead in order to connect with others. I do, however, keep my ears and heart open, making sure that when the opportunity presents itself, I am able to share where I have been and what I have come through or am going through at that moment.

I have been able to share with teens some of the difficulties I faced during my youth and how I worked through them. I have to be willing to share the mistakes I made and pray that they can see the error of my ways and how I am actively striving to be faithful and pleasing to God.

I have shared with wives the fact that submission does *not* come easy for me. I struggle with it regularly, but I'm still hanging in there because I want to be pleasing to God and a blessing to my husband. I've also shared a lot of my mistakes and struggles, praying that I give them hope. Even if it's just, "If that crazy woman can stay married, there's hope for me!" I also pray that they have the strength to make better, more godly decisions than I have made in the past. For example, I have shared with other moms the choices Wayne and I have made in parenting, both good and bad, hoping to lift up other mommas.

Putting your pride aside may require you to share some of your faults, but it also requires you to share your holiness in a way that doesn't center on you, but points instead to Jesus. Sharing with others what has worked for you along your journey is helpful and is but one way we can give encouragement!

Just share you and your experiences. Let the younger generation know that you had your struggles; let them know what they were; let them know that you won in the end. You can give them hope! Show them that you turned out okay.

5. I HAD TO REALIZE WE ARE ALL DIFFERENT!

As a young woman, I was so judgmental! If I could live a busy life with a husband, five children, running a daycare in my home, maintain a strong spiritual life, and a clean house, then others could/should too. Take the whole Tit. 2 passage about older women training the younger women to love their husbands and their children, to be sensible, pure, workers at home, kind, and subject to their husbands (ouch). I had a picture in my head of what that should look like. It came from my mom, my mother-in-law, and some of the other godly women in church whom I looked up too.

It wasn't until my children started getting married that I learned to back off. I started looking at other women and realized we would all have different homes. Some would be cleaner than others. Some families would do everything together; some would not. Some marriages would reflect love and respect; some would reflect constant turmoil. It wasn't up to me to decide what their lives should look like. When I realized that we all come from different backgrounds, are married to different people, and have different priorities, it changed the way I looked at others. I prayed for patience and understanding so that I would be capable of encouraging them, even when they were "different" from me. I prayed that I would let go of my preconceived ideas and love them *because* they are different. Now I love the fact that we are all different and bring different personalities into the body (Eph. 4:11-16). Wouldn't it be boring if we were all alike? Who wants to be a Stepford wife!?

I also had to realize that most women are *petrified* of opening up to another Christian for fear of being judged. Because of that fear, they are turning to the world for advice, and that is exactly what they are getting: worldly advice. We must realize that we are all different and will have different struggles. Just because someone else's struggles seem "worse" than your own does not make it more sinful than yours. Be there for those that seem different from you, and you will be blessed by them!

6. I HAD TO START LISTENING!

I realized that if I wanted someone to listen to me, I had to start listening to them first (Prov. 10:19; 15:23, 28; 18:2). I was so focused on what I was going to say and how I was going to help others that I wasn't even hearing what their needs actually were.

I have always been a talker. If you needed a spokesperson for anything, I was your go-to girl! If there was a question asked in class, my hand went up. Usually my mouth opened before the hand went up. People liked me; I was the life of the party! So when I realized I wasn't really connecting with people, I had to ask myself; Why? I came to the epiphany that I wasn't taking the time to let them speak. I wasn't truly getting to know them. I learned it was time for me to hush!

So many times, women just need someone to talk to. They need a listening ear that isn't trying to fix all of their problems—they have a husband who is doing his best with that job!

7. I SAW A NEED TO REMAIN POSITIVE!

I am a social media person. I will get on Facebook and go to one of many group sites, which I will not name to avoid hurting any feelings. I start reading through the posts and get discouraged. So many women are such complainers. They spend so much of their venting time (you know what I'm talking about!) on sharing their woes. I will not be that person! My life is overflowing with blessings and I will *not* be bogged down in the messy stuff! Women need you to show them that your joy, as well as their own, has been made full (John 15:11).

Don't get me wrong; I realize we all have our down days. We all hurt and need someone to talk to. I get that. I have people that I turn to when I need prayers. Instead, I'm talking about your overall attitude.

When Wayne first became a preacher, I had another, older preacher's wife share with me how to prepare myself for the journey ahead. She painted a bleak and negative picture. All I could think was, "That sounds awful." I have come to realize that it is all about your attitude. So if a young preacher's wife comes to me, I *lift her up*! I try to defuse the negative and point to the positive. Isn't that who we are supposed to be anyway?

8. I HAD TO CONTINUE TO GROW!

I also have to *continually* ask for wisdom (Jas. 1:5). These women are asking all kinds of questions and truly need someone to help them. The Lord's body has so many hurts and struggles. I have to stay within the Word in order to be equipped to answer from the Word (2 Tim. 3:16-17; Col. 4:2-4). I also have to stay within the Word for me to stay filled up so that I can continue (Psa. 19:7-8).

I watch for any other opportunities to grow. I speak/teach when I am asked. I attend ladies' days and ladies' retreats, even when I'm not the speaker. I take classes if they are available. I sit at the feet of other women. I spend time with Christian women and with those walking in the light. Their light is contagious! I remember that every day is a do over! I can start fresh every day, renewing myself so that I can refresh others (Philem. 1:7).

So, what is my answer to the question, "Is anyone listening?" They sure are! There are women out there starving to hear from you. Be patient and pray! Open your eyes to the opportunities! These women are just waiting on you to look up and see them. Just be you when you finally do look up! They are going to love who you are. They are going to love you for what you have come through and because you love the Lord. They are going to love you because you love them! Embrace their differences; encourage their differences! Show them the joy you have in Christ Jesus! "Is anyone listening?" Yes! And it needs to be you!

Go, listen to them. You'll be surprised at how much you grow!

10

YOUR RELATIONSHIP WITH CHRIST
Ashley Hudson

I sat in my car at the edge of Lake Hefner, wanting to drive myself into it. Sweat from my back soaked my shirt. Salty tears streaked my face. My knuckles ached as I gripped the steering wheel. I never thought I would hit rock bottom...again. I sat drenched in an outpour of bitterness and defeat, wanting to coward out of life. I didn't want to be the youth intern's wife anymore. I didn't want to continue to pretend I was holy. I didn't want to keep searching for the man I married pre-deployment.

I allowed myself to become distastefully bitter towards my husband. He was supposed to cherish me. Honor me. Rescue me. Teach me. He was supposed to be my protector and guardian—an image of perfection, especially if he wanted to be a preacher! I prayed like a child before her father, ready to tattle-tale. I spilled all of his wrongs, the damage he caused, and why I wanted just to be done. Hours slipped away, and tears continued to fall. The Lord was preparing me to realize that the hole in my soul had nothing to do with the man I was struggling to love, and everything to do with me and the relationship I had abandoned with Christ.

I opened my eyes after hours of having them shut. The light stung. I could barely focus on the images before me due to my pupils trying to adjust to the sudden burst of light refracting off my unshed tears. The sun was setting. It had been right overhead before I started praying, and now it was falling off into the water. The lake shimmered with beautiful hues of orange, pink, and purple. Clouds were positioned just right to make fractions of prisms burst forth from them, as if the glory of God was demanding my attention. As I put my car in drive, a thought came to my mind.

"You shall have no other gods before me."

I put my car back into park. "Psssh!" I mumbled under my breath, feeling like a lunatic. "I'm not putting any other gods before you, Lord! I have spent these past two years growing closer and closer to you! When Jake left for Egypt, I clung to you, spent hours in prayer over my marriage, future, and purpose. I filled my heart each day with your Word. Jake did too! We decided to go into ministry and share your love with others. Nothing is before you, Lord!" I felt satisfied with that. I reflected back on the phone call Jake and I shared while he was in Egypt.

Jake: "Ashley, I have to tell you something, and you may think I'm crazy, but when I come back, I do not want to be an Ag teacher anymore."

Me: "Ok, what would you like to do? Don't say another deployment...I will hurt you."

Jake: "No, I want to be a youth minister."

Silence.

Jake: "Hello?"

Me: "A youth minister!? That's amazing, but why?"

Jake: "Because I have taken my life for granted until this

point. The people over here are begging for Bibles. Bibles are considered contraband, and they can die for having one! They don't care; they risk it because they believe in it. I want that. I want to help others know God."

I was so excited to hear this. I hated him being away, but felt it was the best thing to happen to his soul and mine. He was truly discovering God for the first time in his life, and I was too.

The excitement of the journey that was before us made the lonely nights without my husband more bearable. I talked to God all the time. I read over and over again all the amazing Scriptures that I had learned as a child, only to relearn them as an adult. They took on new meaning now that I was grown up. Jake finally came home, and as soon as his boots hit Oklahoma soil, we packed up and moved to Oklahoma City. I called my old youth minister, told him about Jake's decision, and asked what we needed to do. He ended up getting Jake his first internship and connected him to a guidance counselor at Oklahoma Christian University. We did it. Jake was in college studying ministry and eventually became a youth intern. We busied ourselves with getting to know each other again after his deployment, but with the additional strain of school, work, our daughter, bills, church functions, teen gatherings, moving, etc, it was a lot to take on for a couple of 20-year-olds. We were barely more than kids ourselves.

I was so proud of my husband. He had several issues getting acclimated back into society after his deployment, but he overcame each of them day-by-day. Seeing him study, watching him grow and mature as a Christian, and receive guidance from his mentors was a joyful experience. He was forming relationships with godly people and with God himself. I was in awe of Jake. He was passionately putting on the armor of God. I wasn't studying or praying as much; I had an apartment to keep clean, a husband to support financially, and an impossible budget to maintain. I tried to piggy-back off Jake's studies. I would proofread his papers or ask him to tell me what he talked about in class that day. I asked him if we could study as a couple and hold me accountable because of my lack of effort. He did—for a while. But his homework was brutal, so we took a break, and without him studying with me, I didn't want to do it anymore.

Time slipped by and tension began to brew. I became bitter because he was taking care of everyone else's spiritual needs, but not bothering with mine. I willed myself to be a better wife and tried to make this possible. It didn't work. I kept failing him. He kept failing me. The fire that had ignited us to serve the Lord together had gone out. We didn't pray together. We didn't study together. We didn't serve together. We were too busy trying to get him into ministry to bother with those things. I was too busy worrying about my marriage and life in general to bother with my personal prayer and study. I stopped eating and became severely depressed.

All of these things brought me to the lake to contemplate living that day. I didn't understand why a couple who wanted to share God's love with teenagers found themselves so far from feeling the same love for themselves.

"You shall have no other gods before me."

I sought comfort in Jake. Joy came from how he made me feel. My spiritual well being was in his hands. I replaced Christ with my husband. I stopped pursuing the eternal and grabbed hold of the superficial. I isolated myself from my Savior. I was so invested in placing my energy in my husband that I lost my connection with Christ. I made a godly man my god. I placed him on a pedestal that completely blocked the view of my Savior. He didn't ask to be placed there. He didn't want to be there. He was new to Christianity and was struggling as well. During this point in his life, he had a wife who expected too much as soon as he came up from the waters of baptism. I tied a brick around his emotions and dropped it into a sea of unhealthy expectations.

Finally, a breakthrough began. I was empty because I lost my first love. I asked God to help me tear down the idol I had created and help me put Christ back where he belonged. I asked him to help me understand where Jake belonged. I grabbed a napkin and wrote down all the things that I—not Jake—needed to work on to enhance my relationship with Christ, and thanked God for yet another chance gifted to me during a rock-bottom moment.

After hours of prayer, I realized what was missing and understood the void that needed to be filled. I left the lake crowned in transcendent peace. I came home to find Jake pacing the floor. He promised to work on the darkness in his life, and I promised to work on mine. The tool I had been using to etch out my idol was dropped from my hands, and I saw my husband as God saw him. A child of God. A piece of clay, longing to be formed by the Potter. He was just like me. A brother in Christ needing nothing more than a helpmeet to work alongside him in a fallen world.

Realizing that I was making an idol in my life is what brought me to the relationship I have today with Christ. Eternity hinges on our relationship with him. You want to give everything to the man you work alongside, are intimate with, and admire—the one who edifies you and encourages you. If you do this, however— if you give him everything—you're missing out on a Man even greater than your husband. You are missing out on the Man who, along with his Father, purposed your life from the very beginning. He knows your story and helps shape it. He desires you to be his. He chose the cross because he knew his death was worth it. It brought him to you. And he wants all of you. I lost track of eternity when I pursued my husband over my Savior.

To truly experience a deep relationship with Christ, we must push our idols aside daily. Yes, I said daily. I may have taken down the idol I made of my husband, but later I put him right back on the pedestal again. Then I swapped him out for my kids, for photography, for deadlines, then for church work. I always seem to have this imaginary pedestal full of carved images that I continue to put before my relationship with Christ. Striving for this relationship is never easy. There is always a constant barrage of things vying for your attention. But sister, struggling for this relationship is so worth it. Jesus is so worth it.

When we take the idols down, we feel empowered, because Christ is filling us with his presence (2 Cor. 4:6-7). We sometimes forget this righteousness is of God, not of ourselves. If it's from ourselves, then we become prideful (Eph. 2:9). To stay connected with Christ, we must understand our ability to remain broken. In his Sermon on the Mount, Jesus told the people, "'Blessed are the poor in spirit, for theirs is the kingdom of heaven" (Matt. 5:3). The word "poor" in this context refers to those who are powerless. It talks about being someone who is completely helpless without the assistance of an outside source. Filling our hearts with Jesus can make us prideful because we often feel we are the ones with the power, not Christ. We strive for a superwoman-like status, forgetting the broken vessel we are meant to remain, especially as minister's wives.

I fought this battle of pride vs. poverty when we made our move to another congregation for my husband's next job. He became the associate minister for a small congregation full of gray-haired people. We loved it. I got busy with projects. I cooked for the sick and wrote cards. I visited people in the hospital and the nursing home. I attended all the potlucks with my best dishes. I spiffed up my outward appearance so I could impress those who worshipped with me. I excelled at being a minister's wife on the outside. Yet, I became the dirty cup Jesus spoke of in Luke 11:39. I made it about me and did what I thought was expected of me. Worship was a routine. Bible class was a checkmark off the schedule. Good deeds made me look good. Instead of fanning the Spirit's fire within me, I focused on fanning my image. The minister's wife at the time, Robyn (one of my greatest mentors), saw right through my act and helped me through it. This sweet sister was constantly helping me keep my focus on the *why* of service. She helped keep my intentions in line with my love for the Lord, not with the pacification of people. I love her so dearly for this.

Soon, the internship was over and our families said their goodbyes. Robyn slipped me a piece of paper and said in her African accent, "I'm terrible with goodbyes, so here—read this, and remember it. Goodbye." It read: "Know who you are. Know what you're striving for. Know who you are trying to please."

You are a child of God, an ambassador for Christ. You are striving to share his love with all. You do this, not to appease the masses and fit into a nice little minister's wife package— you do these things to please Jesus and expand his presence in your heart. Being authentic in your service strengthens Christ in you and solidifies your relationship with him. A people-pleasing heart leaves no room for a spirit meant to take the state of dependence. A dependent heart, a poor heart, is always grasping for Jesus. Understanding this will create a thankful heart that serves others because it praises the source of its strength.

Finally, my sister, remember the Holy Spirit. Feeling as if I still have much to learn about the works of the Spirit, I can share with you only two things. The Spirit will guide your mind, and the Spirit will share in your prayers.

On several occasions, I have found myself in a closet with a bag full of Reese's. I go there when things rest heavy on my heart and I simply can't shake them. I wrap myself in darkness, pretending it is the embrace of my heavenly Father. I allow my tears to do the talking. Each tear running down my face represents sorrow and groaning too deep for words (Rom. 8:26). These prayers are not filled with "fix this" or "help that"— they are just release. I feel like Hannah leaving all her sorrows at the feet of her Lord, but not looking back. We tend to forget the awesome power of prayer. We turn it into a routine or duty because we know it is something we are supposed to do. We have been taught that the key to a good relationship with God consists of prayer, meditation, and Bible study, yet we make these vital things mundane. We forget the power of the Spirit inside us. In fact, we barely acknowledge him at all. Jesus left an amazing piece of himself within us, and we neglect it's power. When you pray, remember the Spirit inside of you; get him involved in each word, feeling, and moment.

The Spirit also wants to be involved in your decisions and help you make the best ones. If you feel the need to make a phone call to check in on someone, acknowledge the Spirit. When words do not come easily while you try to comfort a friend, take it as the Spirit giving you an opportunity just to be present so that God can be felt through those who hurt. When comforting whispers of Scripture are permeating through your heart in times of desperation, understand the Holy Spirit is stirring. Feed on those Words; speak those Words. When a plan comes together to glorify God in unlikely ways, know the Spirit is infused within you. Never be ashamed of this miraculous relationship for fear of sounding too charismatic.

Let's go back to the beginning of my story when I was sitting in the car. I prayed to God for comfort, whining to him about what was wrong. The Word of God, sharper than a sword, pierced through my heart at that moment: "You shall have no other gods before me" (Exod. 20:3). It was precisely what I needed to hear at that moment. The Spirit gave the apostles the right words just when they needed them (Luke 12:12). We should understand that this is still true for us today. The way the Lord gave the apostles words through miraculous workings was different than what we have today, but it remains just as powerful. The Spirit gives us these words when we need them most. He gives us strength, comfort, joy, and hope in his Word. Moreover, these life-altering Words are not confined to the pages of a book. When we speak or hear them—when we believe in them—they become one with our souls, and the Spirit injects our being with its power.

Disregard coincidence; leave room for the Spirit's stirring. When you allow stillness to permeate your heart and mind, the fire within you will ignite your soul. It will leave you craving more of his presence. The pedestal you place your revolving idols upon will crumble. Your time in the Word will become a feast. Your service will flourish and bring God total glory. Your prayer life will become as vital as breathing. You are given the wonderful responsibility of being a minister's wife, but remember that there is no specific formula in the Bible we are meant to follow while in this role. Trust me—I checked!

We are only asked to be a faithful child of God, an ambassador of Christ, a helpmeet to our men, and a wise mother of the home. Don't get pulled away from the greatest relationship you will ever know because of someone else's assumptions of how a minister's wife should look, talk, and act. Pursue your relationship with Christ with fervor, and the rest will fall into place. As Christian women, we will each experience life in different ways and take different paths, but our end goal is the same. We just want Jesus.

To God be the glory forever and ever.

ABOUT THE AUTHORS

DONNA FAUGHN is the wife of Jim Faughn, minister and one of the elders of the Central church of Christ in Paducah, KY. They have two adult children and five grandchildren. Donna attended Southern Illinois University and has a degree in Communication. She taught Speech and English on the high school and junior college level. Donna is a very active preacher's/elder's wife who enjoys teaching ladies' classes, speaking at ladies' days and lectureships, reading, and decorating her home.

KATHY POLLARD is a graduate of Faulkner University. Her husband, Neal, preaches for the Bear Valley church of Christ in Denver, CO. They have three sons—Gary, Dale, and Carl. Kathy is an instructor in the Women's Program at the Bear Valley Bible Institute International, a director of Higher Ground (a Bible camp for teen girls), and the author of *Return to Me: What to Do When Loved Ones Fall Away*.

LEA MORGAN is a minister's wife and mother to four boys. Lea and her husband, Trey, have been doing ministry together since they married in 1988. They are currently working with the Childress, TX Church of Christ. They have developed "Trey & Lea's Stronger Marriage Workshops" and travel all over speaking to couples about how to have healthy, godly marriages.

MELANIE JENKINS is a graduate of Freed-Hardeman University. She and her husband, Dale, have two sons who are both youth ministers, as well as three precious grandchildren. Dale preaches for the Spring Meadows Church of Christ in Spring Hill, TN. Melanie is the office manager at Spring Hill Eyecare.

BEVERLY WATKINS is the daughter of a preacher, the sister of a preacher, the daughter-in-law of a preacher, the sister-in-law of a preacher, and the wife of a preacher. Beverly and her husband, Bill, have been married for 43 years. Bill preaches for the Crieve Hall Church of Christ in Nashville, TN. Together, they have five children and twenty-two grandchildren. Beverly loves reading, camping, walking, and being with her family.

KATHY HAYNES has been married to Tommy since 1978, and they have three grown children and six grandchildren. After serving congregations in Scurry, Farmersville, and San Saba, TX, they moved to Oklahoma in 1987 to work with the Central Church of Christ in Moore. Kathy coordinates and teaches Time Travelers, a children's Bible class program for three-year-olds through third-grade students. She is an elementary school teacher, teaching English as a second language.

JUDI DEAN was raised on a farm in North Carolina. She has been married for 36 years to Stan Dean, minister for the Killen Church of Christ in Killen, AL. They have three children and seven grandchildren. Judi is co-author of *Sweet Truths* with her sister, Cynthia Guy. Judi enjoys teaching Bible classes and speaking at ladies' days and retreats. She especially enjoys being a minister's wife with all its blessings!

CARRIE VOSS met her husband, John, at Freed-Hardeman University, and they have been married for fifteen years. John preaches for the Eagle Way Church of Christ in Hopkinsville, KY. They have one daughter, Emily. Carrie has helped organize the annual preachers' wives retreat held each spring and has spoken several times for ladies' classes at Polishing the Pulpit.

TAMI ROBERTS and her husband, Wayne, travel around the country sharing their marriage seminar, "His Shoes, Her Shoes." Tami is the co-founder of the Come Fill Your Cup web site for women and puts together their annual spring Spiritual Development Retreat outside of Denver. She and Wayne have raised five children and are enjoying six grandchildren. They live in California where Wayne currently serves as the Family and Outreach minister for the Ripon Church of Christ.

ASHLEY HUDSON lives in Madill, OK where she is a preacher's wife, mother to three, and an avid coffee lover. She enjoys writing, blogging, and sharing in the joys of the power of the gospel, unity, discount shopping, football, and crockpot cooking. She speaks regularly at ladies' days and teen conferences. Her blog, "There's an App for That," can be read each week at Start2Finish; her writing has also been featured in *Christian Woman* and *Think*.

77243526R00072

Made in the USA
Columbia, SC
26 September 2017